"Tami Lynn Kent has written an inspiring guide for calling forth the creative energies that transform daily experience into a soulful adventure that is wildly alive and deeply fulfilling."

—**Donna Eden**, author of *Energy Medicine*

"An inspiring analysis of creativity and wholeness from one of the most pioneering gurus of the mind-body connection in women."

—**Naomi Wolf**, author of *Vagina: A New Biography*

"Tami's wonderfully wild book presents a clear model for the creative field, a three-fold energetic field that enables us to flow into our dreams—and flow our dreams into our everyday lives. After reading *Wild Creative*, I asked myself: What dream-wings am I wearing and where might I meet an eagle at the water's edge? By merging our truest masculine and feminine aspects, we can (finally) create our truest lives—and selves."

—**Cyndi Dale**, intuitive, energy healer and author of *The Subtle Body*

"*Wild Creative* is the medicine that we all need to restore our power, spirit, and joy in everyday life. This book will teach you to build an energetic framework matching the potency of your soul."

—**Christiane Northrup, MD**, author of *Women's Bodies, Women's Wisdom*

Wild Creative

Igniting Your Passion and Potential in Work, Home, and Life

Tami Lynn Kent

ATRIA PAPERBACK
New York London Toronto Sydney New Delhi

BEYOND WORDS
Hillsboro, Oregon

ATRIA PAPERBACK
A Division of Simon & Schuster, Inc.
1230 Avenue of the Americas
New York, NY 10020

BEYOND WORDS
20827 N.W. Cornell Road, Suite 500
Hillsboro, Oregon 97124-9808
503-531-8700 / 503-531-8773 fax
www.beyondword.com

Managing editor: Lindsay S. Brown
Editors: Jenefer Angell
Copyeditor: Meadowlark Publishing Services
Proofreader: Jennifer Weaver-Neist
Design: Devon Smith
Composition: William H. Brunson Typography Services

First Atria Paperback/Beyond Words trade paperback edition August 2014

Library of Congress Cataloging-in-Publication Data

Kent, Tami Lynn.
    Wild creative : igniting your passion and potential in work, home, and life / Tami Lynn Kent.
        pages cm
    1. Creative ability.   2. Creative ability in business.   3. Creative thinking.   I. Title.
    BF408.K444   2014
    153.3'5—dc23

                                                                                2014003938

ISBN 978-1-58270-355-8
ISBN 978-1-4516-6854-4 (ebook)

To all the wild creatives—
the world needs you to dream
and to bring your dreams to life.

CONTENTS

Dear Reader,

I invite you to journey into the creative field—the place between spirit and body where the energy to manifest your dreams resides. Your creative field is perfectly designed for making your best life, but there is little guidance for knowing how to access this place. In working with thousands of women (and, increasingly, the men in their lives), I've found that happiness and energy health is related to creative expression. The ability to attune with one's inner creative landscape is a direct measure of one's creative abundance. And this ability can be cultivated with practice.

Whether you want to discover your creativity now or you already feel creative but desire to increase this potential, this book contains energy meditations, stories, and hands-on tools. It reveals a framework for understanding and expanding the multidimensional aspects of creative expression across the range of your life.

You are inherently creative. Your creative energy is relevant and essential for bringing your dreams into being. May you know the power, spirit, and joy of your wild creative range.

OPENING

Meeting the Wild

Summer showed itself in the brightness of the morning sun. This day, something called my spirit out of its slumber and beckoned me to venture forth in a bold and unchartered way.

Seeking to share the essence of the land where we live with our sons, my husband and I deliberately go to the wild places in our city. We take our sons to witness what we have learned by connecting with the wild; for us, wild places offer the most direct access to spirit. By meeting spirit in the wild and opening ourselves to the possibility in a given moment, we tend to its presence in our lives naturally, finding a deep satisfaction as we do so.

On this day, since Dan was working, the boys and I went to the wild on our own. I needed the medicine that only an encounter with spirit could provide.

I was pondering several fundamental questions: How can we live in relationship to the wild when many of our modern structures lead us away from its inherent nature? How can we follow a creative path without simply chasing one whim or another? How can we find our sense of order without diminishing the wild, creative movement of spirit? How do we keep the creative fires burning even as we develop a profession, make an income, or balance the needs of work and home? How, then, do we maintain our soulfulness and spontaneity while fulfilling the need for planning and form that inhabiting a daily life requires? And how can I nurture my own creative life in the midst of mothering my children? To experience the wild and alive energy we yearn for involves knowing how to follow our inspiration as we make a structure to contain it.

To *inspire* is to be *filled with spirit*. If we make our inspiration a priority and recognize it as a movement that occurs in the process of following spirit, a small miracle unfolds. We rediscover an energy current that is inherently ours—the root pulse of every living being and life cycle. In seeking our inspiration, we realign ourselves with an ancient presence and reawaken the *wild creative* within. We begin to see more clearly with this part of ourselves intact.

I needed the wild beyond the city, so my sons and I set off to a place where our city's river crosses coastal mountains to join the Pacific Ocean. We traveled farther to immerse ourselves in the energetic potential of nature. Accepting an invitation to explore new territory by making a spontaneous trip to the beach meant surrendering to the potential of the unknown. We left the bright sun and journeyed toward a changing sky, arriving at the mouth of a mighty river. Wind slapped the water and threw sand into the air. I drew my children close to me, and together we waded through water-laced gusts. We walked the narrow strip of beach and sheltered in the shadow of a giant driftwood tree. Quiet descended over us as we settled into our surroundings.

In this momentary peace, I could see the truth of my present life: I was at the end of a particular trail. I had followed in faith the path of my life so far as healer, mother, and writer—and had come to an impasse. I had the beginnings of a manuscript, but the book I was writing could not find a publisher. My husband and I were struggling financially with the highly unpaid work of tending two young children and jobs that were not yet enough to sustain us. In the midst of mothering and working, I hungered for a tangible and meaningful mode of creative expression. I knew this, but I had no idea what to do in response.

So here I was in the wild. Sitting in the sand, laden with despair, I called out to spirit: *I have traveled this way in faith, but there is no clear direction from here. I am lost. SPIRIT, I NEED YOUR HELP.*

As if in response, the water began to drum against the shore, speaking in her native tongue. My eldest son, then four years old, said: "Mama, it's talking to us!" I sat up straight, alert. The water pounded a clear rhythm. It was then that my wild self sensed something my mind only registered later.

An eagle met us at the water's edge.

A raven called from the driftwood tree, perched on a branch worn smooth by its time at sea. I turned my head in the direction of the call in time to register the eagle's shape, flying low above the sandy shore. I watched each graceful wing stroke that drew it still nearer to where we sat, as if bound just for us. I felt the energy field surrounding my whole being expand, as if my body and my boys and the river and the eagle were all one. The eagle flew past our place in the sand as if we were simply a rock or tree. In that moment when our breath became wind, we were.

There is a vitality, a life force, an energy, a quickening
that is translated through you into action, and because there is
only one of you in all of time, this expression is unique . . . .
It is not your business to determine how good it is,
Nor how valuable, or how it compares with other expressions.
It is your business to keep it yours clearly and directly,
to keep the channel open.

—MARTHA GRAHAM

You must learn one thing.
The world was made to be free in.
Give up all the other worlds
except the one to which you belong.

—DAVID WHYTE
"SWEET DARKNESS"[1]

Awakening Your Creative Soul

*The intuitive mind is a sacred gift, and the rational mind is a
faithful servant. We have created a society that honors
the servant and has forgotten the gift.*

—ALBERT EINSTEIN

My most important callings are to be mother and healer, and increasingly, the work I do in both places seems connected to this: restoring people's connection to the creative field and keeping it alive in the midst of living. As a healer, I began as a women's health physical therapist, fixing problems in the pelvic bowl—but the body overall taught me much more. Once I learned to listen, the body had many answers for the spirit of the person with whom I was working: namely, how to rekindle the inner creative fire and how essential that fire is for life.

My encounter with the eagle in response to my call to spirit placed me directly in touch with my inner connection to the sacred. I went to the wild seeking answers about the outer world, but the wild reflected back to me the essence of my own soul. We all have the capacity to commune with spirit, but when everyday life doesn't allow for connection to the wild—and the wild within—we easily lose our access to this still point as essential guide, gauge, and source for living and building the life of our dreams. And though a miracle, like my experience with the eagle, may joyfully remind us of the profound nature of our existence, the truth is that this capacity always lies within us; we don't need a miracle to find it. We only need to remember our way back to our wild creative selves and the ancient energy we already contain.

Around your physical core are your body's energy field and the energy imprints that define and give shape to your creative range. This is your *creative-energy field* or *framework*, and it determines how creative energy flows as a current in your body and life—both where it flows and how abundantly.

Beyond the energy layer is the realm of spirit and ancestor, the mystery that moves through and around you and that can exponentially expand your creative potential. Altogether, the physical, energetic, and spiritual layers reveal how you inhabit your creative field, which is unique to you but also a part of the greater creative-energy field, the source of all inspiration.

A four-month-old child came into my office recently with his mother, and I was struck by the wholeness of his creative field: all he knew was full embodiment of his potential. Yet in our linear pursuits, most of us have lost touch with this inner creative field. To restore wholeness in ourselves, we need to come back to this original creative channel. Using the creative field to cultivate physical and energetic alignment, we can optimize the creative-energy potential that can then flow more readily into our bodies and lives.

This book is a call back to your creative center and the beauty contained there; may it reawaken in you a sense of wonder. Creativity nourishes your soul and supports a vibrant, radiant expression of your life force. Too many dreams have been cast aside in the pursuit of a career or financial security, based on a formula of success as written by the societal pressures of the "rational mind." Yet deep and lasting happiness requires expression of the soul—and not in between the tasks of one's working life but as a fundamental way of being.

To begin awakening your inherently creative soul, ask yourself:

- Are you in touch with your creativity and creative potential?
- Are you overly task oriented, or do you allow yourself open time and pleasure?
- Is your life and the way you spend most of your days satisfying?
- Can you name your top dreams right now? And do you know how to realize your dreams in the various facets of your life?
- Are some parts of your life flowing while it seems like you cannot make things happen the way you desire in other parts?
- Do you feel deeply fulfilled, or are you still yearning for something that is difficult to name?

If you are satisfied with your answers to these questions, you are on the right track for living creatively. If not, your life may need a boost from the energy contained in your creative-energy field.

If you want more ways to embrace the fullness of your inner creative potential or have a creative dream you would like to bring to fruition, this book is for you. And because every person's path is unique, instead of containing a single prescription, this book teaches you how to reconnect with your creative center and follow the guidance within that has direct relevance to your creative life. It reveals hidden obstacles that often block creative success; it contains tools for realigning the energy framework and turning barriers into resources to expand your creative capacity; and it invites you on a journey to explore this creative range for yourself. Anyone who lives creatively will tell you that it is not always easy and flowing; there are techniques for navigating the currents. Instead of answering "Am I creative or not?" this book suggests that you hone your creative practice and sort through what is revealed in the process. As poet and philosopher David Whyte writes, "There is no possibility of pursuing a work without coming to terms with all the ways it is impossible to do it. Feeling far away from what we want tells us one of two things about our work: that we are at the beginning or that we have forgotten where we are going."[2]

The Essence of Creativity

The truth is that every person is inherently creative. One of the greatest obstacles to living a creative life is not believing that we are. Because artistic talent and creativity are often paired, unless they have a visible, socially valued talent, many people learn to perceive themselves as lacking creativity. Rather than understanding creativity as an energy that every one of us can tap into, you may believe that people either have it or they don't. It is because of constricted ideas about the nature of creativity that many people count themselves out as noncreative.

On a deep level, creativity is a practice of engagement with the *chi*, or life essence, that flows in and around us and through all things. It is a way of being more fully alive by attuning to the natural creative flow in the body and moving in the direction it inspires. If you recognize that you are part of the creative movement, you can begin to use this capacity in all you do to create a life that is infused with this vibrant energy.

Most of our current work and life structures have been devised to emphasize production and how much we can accomplish rather than the nurturing of the soul. This routinely takes us away from our natural inclinations and the flow of our energy field. Therefore, from an early age, we learn how to be productive by finishing assignments, working our way through school, achieving degrees, building careers, buying houses and other goods, making money, and crossing off the items on life's big to-do lists.

Meanwhile, our health and our happiness often suffer. The nonstop emphasis on production leads to the development and honing of skills that are deemed productive rather than those that foster our inner creativity or living from the impulses of our center. However, the problem is not solely with the emphasis on productivity itself; creativity can be immensely productive. The problem is that, generally, our productivity is a habit of keeping busy with prescribed activities without a clear connection to our passions and desires, which naturally energize our body's creative field and produce long-term happiness and fulfillment.

If we connect first with our creative center—the natural, creative-energy field that is our birthright—and allow our productivity to arise from there, the very nature of production changes. Like the seasons, our creativity has cycles that are meant to replenish us after an intensely creative period. Rest, such as napping, taking breaks, or simply allowing the energy around the body to be more spacious, becomes a priority in order to refill the creative center in ourselves. If we know how to cultivate the energy of creativity, we can manifest our life from this place. And if we understand that following a creative rhythm differs from incessant productivity, we will know when we are in the midst of our natural creative flow.

When I have a long list of things to do, even creative tasks, the list itself can be oppressive, blocking creative energy. If I start the tasks from a place of resistance, then my first goal is to change that energy. Rather than focus on what needs to be done on a given day, I follow the guidance from within my own center. For me, I know that taking a walk in the neighborhood, stopping to talk with a friend or neighbor, joining my kids in their play, and sitting in the sun as it warms my body are all ways to reinvigorate the creative well before setting to work on specific tasks. Rather than defining my movements by an external list, I follow my inner creative flow toward a particular inspiration. The energy guides my focus and process.

The organic rhythms that reveal themselves when we attune to our own energy current are far more inspirational than trudging through a list of tasks, yet most of us have learned to ignore these natural impulses because we fear that we won't be productive. Following the inner flow ensures that your internal realm is being nourished even as you are producing, and productivity arises in a more holistic manner.

Creativity is an asset intended for daily use. Whether you are just now reclaiming your own creative essence or you are simply cultivating it more fully, creativity enhances both your productivity and your ability to enjoy the journey. And because there is less job security than there used to be in lifetime careers and less adherence to traditional roles, creative skill sets are being called forth and are more highly valued. This is a time of opportunity for those who have honed their inner wild creative.

Wild creative skills will help you in:

- Expanding your self-expression
- Moving beyond linear pathways toward wholeness
- Reinventing your career path
- Creating a home–work flow
- Inspiring new work or an entrepreneurial venture
- Establishing a creative practice and creative-energy flow
- Bringing inspiration into any aspect of life
- Enhancing the connection between the spirit and body, dreams and manifesting
- Redefining creative partnerships
- Navigating times of challenge or change
- Addressing creative stagnation or blocks
- Employing your full creative potential

Returning to your center—and living from this powerful place—is what it means to be a wild creative.

Your Creative Path through This Book

In my work to restore alignment in the creative energy of the pelvis (as a women's health physical therapist and energy intuitive), I wrote my first book, *Wild Feminine*, about tapping into the feminine aspect of this inner landscape in the female body. This book, *Wild Creative*, is its wild masculine partner. The feminine realm is far more than a gender construct: it is a place of pure inspiration and intuition. This book gives voice to the next phase of this work—taking the raw energy from the feminine and fusing it with the masculine to make dynamic new forms for living an inspired life.

Forms are the daily structures, from work schedules to partnerships, that define our lives. Dynamic forms are responsive rather than rigidly defined, allowing you to align with the creative flow in your center on a given day and then alter these forms in response to flow. Dynamic forms arise from allowing your inspiration to take shape in your world—perhaps in the form of work infused with passion, flexible work schedules, life goals that include the health of the soul, and strategic but still heart-inspired creations. Our modern forms are typically more rigid in nature, lacking room for the creative spirit.

In *New Self, New World: Recovering Our Senses in the Twenty-First Century*, author Philip Shepherd reflects on the collective disconnection between our rational minds and the body (or the wild), and the detrimental effects of this on the lives and careers we are making. He relays that the antidote lies in reintegrating the unique intelligence of the rational mind with that of the body, or more intuitive intelligence. In an interview with *The Sun* magazine, he says, "The integration of multiple perspectives into a whole can happen only when, like the astronaut bringing the photo (of Earth) back to Earth, we bring this information back to our pelvic bowl, back to the ground of our being, back to the integrating genius of the female consciousness. The pelvic bowl is the original beggar's bowl: it receives the gifts of the world— of the male perspective—and it integrates them . . . eventually giving birth to insight."[3]

Having spent significant time with the female pelvic bowl in my women's health practice, I've learned about the creative-energy field that maps a person's relationship between the physical realm of the body and the energetic realm, where creative potential exists. This creative field exists not just in the pelvic bowl but around the whole body. It reflects the imprints and intelligence of the pelvic bowl, however, because this is where our body and energy are first created. Though my clients are mostly women, I have worked with men's creative-energy fields as well, which again relate to the pelvic bowl because this is the place where both males and females come into being in a mother's body. I also live in a male household with my husband and three sons, and I bear witness to how contact with the feminine is absolutely essential for tapping their creativity.

I have found that the energy pattern of either fully or only partially inhabiting the creative core is similar for men and women, although expressed in different ways, depending on the careers and roles they choose for themselves. I notice that my acupuncturist, bodyworker, and astrologer—all males—use their feminine fields when they engage in their highly intuitive work. Observing them with my skills as an energy reader, I see that in these intuitive roles, they are inhabiting their whole creative field, drawing upon and integrating the feminine energy with the masculine in the same way that I work with my clients to access the full range of their core energies.

The power of working with this full physical-energetic interface— where energy comes into form—is not only for creating vibrant health but also the dynamic forms that are unique to you. You need not be limited to constructing your world from the rational mind. This book illustrates the many hands-on ways to make a life by constructing these forms with the creative currents meant to move through you as daily sustenance and inspiration. It teaches you to identify core patterns and interact with them in order to change these patterns to realign your inner creative map—your body's physical-energetic interface that influences your life's overall flow. And it details the personal journeys of friends, business owners, clients, and myself, whose stories demonstrate that tapping into one's holistic creative framework serves well-being in every aspect of living.

Chapters 1 and 2 of this book reorient you to the creative flow within—this creative currency that contains untapped potential—and using a creative framework based on this natural flow to realign your body's creative-energy field. Chapters 3 and 4 explore the creative blocks that arise in the process of reclaiming your creative energy, and the potential these blocks contain for tapping into the whole creative field. They also explore the art of establishing a creative practice that can serve as the foundation of a creative life. Chapter 5 contains the spirit-based rhythms of a creative cycle to help you navigate the non-linear aspects of the creative journey, drawing upon the reserves of spirit to reach for your dreams. And chapter 6 shares examples and tools for living creatively, embodying the wild creative as an expression of your sacred nature.

Another physical therapist came to me when she was seeking to build her heathcare business, asking what my "secret" was and saying, "You are a savvy marketer—everyone knows your work." I thought for a moment and then told her that my business success arose not from any particular marketing technique or business strategy but by recovering the authentic flow of energy from my inner wild creative. And the first step to tapping into this flow was to return to my center—the place my children called me to when I first became a mother. But children are really just the canaries that signal the health of our inner realms and heart spaces. When I asked for guidance from spirit at the river's edge, the deeper message I received from an eagle in the wild was *Look within to your own creative core for the answers you seek.* It is worthwhile for all of us to come to this creative core because it contains an abundance of energy for all that we are making.

When you return to the center of your own creative field, your journey becomes less about achieving an outer trajectory to some idealized point and more about the depth of the full experience. This expanded depth is like a nourishing meal: it meets your real hunger in a sustained manner and provides the fuel for producing true abundance.

Masculine and Feminine:
Two Halves of the Creative Whole

In my private healthcare practice, one of the common imbalances I see in my clients' body–energy fields is an overactive masculine energy flow with an absent or diminished feminine energy. Because of the general emphasis on production, achievement, and building a career, we typically learn to create by becoming self-sufficient and actively doing whatever needs to be done. This emphasizes masculine energy and the masculine aspects of the energy field that say "I can do it." Women tend to fuel their energy with sheer willpower rather than feminine inspiration, often depleting their essence, happiness, libido, and so on. Similarly, men's lives can be formed primarily around external financial and professional goals rather than internal desires, often leading to long-term dissatisfaction because the inner realm is so ignored. The feminine is perceived to be weak or irrelevant, when actually, she is the source of our most potent creative insights.

Remember the Feminine; Redefine the Masculine
The important discovery I've made as a holistic healer is that contact with the feminine has direct relevance to being able to create our lives as we wish them to be. When my clients begin to contact the feminine energy in their bodies, their energy field changes in response. It visibly brightens, and they may describe feeling centered or relaxed. When they reach the most balanced point in a session in my office, often containing insight and powerful healing energy, they access the untapped resources of the feminine. But then something else happens: they reshape the masculine aspects of their field. In the session, the feminine–masculine connection changes the overall potential in

their energy field. And when they become more conscious of using the feminine aspect of the energy field in daily living, their core way of inhabiting life shifts entirely—including their masculine means of getting things done.

They have clearer knowledge of what is not working in their daily habits and more perspective about what they want for themselves. They have more ideas for making changes to embody life in new ways— whether in relationship to work, personal goals, daily schedules, health, family life, partnerships, and so on; all of these aspects of life come into sharper focus, as do some of their long-denied dreams and desires for themselves.

I am fascinated by the relationship between the way a person embodies their whole energy field and their creative capacity; and it has influenced my personal journey. I've made changes in my own energy access and found my life transformed as a result. Each aspect of my creative field that I reclaim expands my overall creative range. In *Wild Creative*, I share the personal and professional tools I've developed for rebalancing the core energy field in order to reshape one's health and life.

Presently, the energy foundation that organizes the flow for most people is the out-of-balance masculine model. This model emphasizes constant output and production, competition by driving out the competitor, unsustainable use of resources, linear models, mentally driven processes, and focus on profits. Unbalanced masculine energy is not related to gender; rather, it is a way of using energy that we all tend toward if we have been raised in a production-oriented way. Increasingly, these linear models are less and less relevant, not to mention detrimental to the environment and frequently incompatible with a sustainable life. When production or corporate profit drives the cultural concept of value, the structures made as a result are typically at odds with human, ecological, and community needs.

Because of our focus on linear pathways and production, the holistic and cyclical nature of the feminine has typically been denied for both genders to the detriment of the whole. Taking ownership of one's creative life force is a conscious act to change the focus from exclusively monetary values to modes that value life. Changing this focus has emotional benefits too. By reconnecting with the feminine, men who have been trained through threat of shame to ignore their emotions, to depend on their careers for their whole identities, and to resist gentler impulses can rediscover these realms and the potential they contain. Similarly, by reconnecting with the feminine, women who have been ashamed of their bodies, their emotions, and their desire to be self-directed against cultural norms can find healing and an inner creative reservoir to inspire their next actions.

Reclaiming feminine attributes of receptivity means that, for both men and women, there is room for replenishment instead of simply producing to the point of depletion. There's time for tango, knitting, daydreaming, or exploring nature because building one's creative wealth has value. Using the feminine vision of the whole, it is easier to see that nonstop growth is ultimately destructive to the whole—whether we are referencing a whole person, community, business, or world. Normal growth is not exponential. Growth for growth's sake alone is a cancer. For the health of our communities and ourselves, both men and women must cultivate space for the feminine in their lives. By connecting to our own wild creative, we can redirect this creative essence in new masculine ways toward the passion, people, and inner callings that make a life of meaning.

Employing Feminine Models for Work and Life

Feminine business and life models are based on feminine attributes such as cooperation, service, holistic perspective, heart-driven processes, natural cycles, cyclical production, restoration, flow between output and input, and focus on long-term sustainability. Our culture supports what it perceives as valuable. To be valued as creative beings, we must refocus our creative energies to integrate feminine values. Then we can reinvent the masculine structures that determine our living and working practices, our life's pleasures, and the expression of our dreams.

In my own feminine business model, self-care and downtime are essential to balancing my high-intensity work schedule and healthcare practice. For example, applying feminine principles in a book launch means that instead of traveling the country in a media blitz, I focus on a long-term commitment to building both a local and online audience through an ongoing connection and cultivation with those who are passionate about this holistic medicine I am sharing. A conventional book tour would be as unsustainable for my body as it would be for my family, so I have chosen a different path—a more feminine one.

My business is based on feminine principles, such as holistic medicine and teaching about the feminine potential within. Similarly, my work revolves around my family life, created in a way that nurtures my family and our heart-based living just as my feminine nature has insisted it be nurtured. I rely on my masculine commitment of focus and task orientation to work out business marketing details, outline books, formulate online strategies, build class structures, and organize the overall master schedule—which includes guarding feminine creative space and tending home fires—but the masculine forms I make are guided by an intuitive feminine vision.

More commonly, our personal and professional lives demonstrate an unbalanced masculine approach in which we ask ourselves questions like *How much can I accomplish today? How can I do as much as they are doing? How much income can I make? How much recognition can I receive? How can I make this situation (whatever the linear focus on a particular outcome may be) happen for myself? Why am I failing to make progress? What is my next goal?*

In contrast, when engaging the feminine and redefining the masculine, we ask ourselves questions such as *What is my creative priority right now? Am I in touch with my creative flow? What stage of this creative cycle am I in? How can I cocreate with others? How is the quality of energy in my overall life? How can I restore core alignment before I begin work? Where can I align my core creative field with the greater creative patterns around me? How can I attune with the broader rhythms and resources of spirit? What am I learning or receiving from my inner guidance at this time?*

Nurturing a Creative Cycle in Modern Life

A friend told me about Pema Chödrön, the American author and Tibetan Buddhist nun, and how she takes a year of retreat for herself. She is a well-loved public figure with an active outer life of teaching and writing, yet she makes a wide swath of time and space for quiet, extended meditation. Chödrön's website also mentions that she plans to spend an increasing amount of time in solitary retreat under her teacher's guidance.

A yearlong inner retreat and plans to increase this time are likely to replenish a visible outer public life. Yet how many public figures live this way? Making space for the inner world that is equivalent to the outer world is a true model of a life based on natural rhythms. I translate the old saying *Behind every good man is a good woman* to *Behind every good masculine is a good feminine*. In order to have a robust outer presence (masculine), one must have an equally robust inner presence (feminine), balancing the energy fields and harvesting energy in a sustainable rather than depletive manner.

The creative current moves between both realms: from the feminine, where creative inspiration occurs, to the masculine, which builds it into a specific form. In the same manner, there are periods of outer, visible creativity when the masculine is in full production or harvest mode; but these busy periods are then integrated with the more yin and feminine time of nourishment and restoration, to replenish the energy output. This is the way of the natural world, which is both robustly productive and deeply restorative across every seasonal year. Plants that bear fruit have a seasonal output that alternates with fallow periods; and trees tend to produce one year of abundance that is followed by two to three years of reduced yield. This is how to model a life that draws sustainably from the creative current throughout the seasons.

In periods of stillness and feminine space, both women and men receive inspiration that moves with the freedom of unformed energy. This is plenary inspiration that flows to guide, inspire, and nourish the forms we make for ourselves. Moving toward the masculine, this energy becomes words on the page, specific tasks or ways of being, a particular creation, the outer aspects of tending a family, a career, a piece of land, or a spiritual practice. The energy is transformed from an expansive notion into a specific or focused form. This is the movement of spirit transitioning to body that requires a strong connection to both feminine and masculine fields of energy.

In thinking about creativity over a period of a decade or more, notice that some years are more internal as you work on strengthening what you already have or integrating what you have learned. Each year when I have given birth to a child—or published a book—has been a year filled with the powerful outward movement that comes with a new creation. But prior to these actual and metaphorical births, there is work to build and formulate the creation, and after the birth, to nourish and integrate what was created. Creativity is cyclical, and these creative currents continue to flow within the earth and in our bodies despite the structure of modern life that has buried these natural patterns. Reawakening your awareness to these cycles and learning how to move with them is essential for nurturing the creative flow and a life nourished by this deeper current.

Though we may tend to take note of visibly productive years where we have "something to show" for our work, the less visible years are equally important and essential to the overall creative journey. The time spent on inner processes can repair or remodel the core energy structure from which you are making your life. Taking time to be in the feminine realms, you find layers of expansive rest that will alter your creative framework when you allow yourself to settle into the place of being instead of doing. Allowing—even inviting—the reformation and exploration that occurs in your center when you are present there for an extended period is powerful fuel for doing. You may receive a whole download of insight or inspiration in the energy field as a design for your next phase of creative production.

The way to obtain creative gifts such as wholly formed insight is to readily inhabit the feminine/left energy field that can receive them. Inhabiting this place means making time for it through retreat, travel, naps, dreams, walks, slow meals, deep conversation, meditation, ritual, prayer, nature, cultivation of the wild landscape within, and presence with children, pets, and loved ones. Perhaps we might take Chödrön's example and build in periods of retreat that are greater than or at least equal to our outer lives, knowing that internal movements are a vital part of the full creative cycle and elemental for the creation of a soul-filled life.

ONE

Creativity as Currency

Dwell as near as possible to the channel in which your life flows.
— HENRY DAVID THOREAU

We give voice to the importance of living soulfully and finding our dreams—which is the natural outcome of dwelling near "the channel in which your life flows"—yet the truth is that the modern framework most of us follow through school and professional development tends to lead us far away from that channel. In the process of making a living, we may hardly remember what this channel contains for us.

As a healer, I've witnessed the powerful flow of this channel in the body: In women, the pelvic bowl contains the creative center and the spirit door through which we all enter. For men, the root and pelvic chakras also contain energy potential that can be nurtured through the aligning exercises and meditations in this book. For both genders, creative energy is meant to flow throughout the whole body—both the physical body and the body of one's life. Where is the channel of your life flowing?

Cultural creatives know how to source their lives from the creative channel. One day, I was visiting friends who reside at a colorful intersection in my city. They live on one of four corners that overlook a great sunflower painted on the street, its vividly colored petals stretching

1

from sidewalk to sidewalk. We sat on the porch, gazing down on the sunflower, when a restored 1940s farm truck drove up with a full-size string bass leaning across the back. Esperanza Spalding, the Grammy award–winning musician and jazz singer, was driving the pickup and, we later learned, filming the video for her song "City of Roses," which would win her another Grammy.

We moved to the street to watch the unfolding scene. The video footage was captured in a few minutes, and then Esperanza parked the truck. Standing a few feet from her, I was struck by her radiance. Here was a woman who was completely at ease in the midst of a video shoot—as if the very universe around her held nothing but divine support. She is profoundly talented, and at age twenty, became the youngest professor ever at the Berklee College of Music. Seeing her in person, I could feel the depth of the creative channel she lived from and the way she made full use of it in her energy field. We all have this potential, but some rare individuals do it so naturally that it is worth watching and learning from them.

Though hesitant to disturb her flow, I asked her a question about a Portland jazz program she had attended, wondering if it was a possibility for my own musically gifted son. She leaned into my question with the same skillful ease she carried throughout her energy field, answering in words—but I swear I heard music. The type of embodied grace that Esperanza exudes is the potential. Listen to her music, watch her on video, see a performance, feel what she is modeling; and then fine-tune your own creative channel. You don't have to be Esperanza to align with the creative genius in your own energy field, but you do have to come back to your own center and live in this flow.

Creative Currency: The Channel of Your Life Flow

The first key to reclaiming your creative abundance is to find your creative currency: the channel or flow that feeds your energy field. It could be exercise, gardening, cooking, dancing, journaling, fishing, playing a sport, or gathering with friends. It does not matter what it is, and you do not have to be able to make a living with it. Your creative currency is the thing or things that feed your soul and make you feel tangibly alive; it is the channel in which your life is meant to flow. Dwelling near it, you return to what is essential for you.

In order to define your creative channel, think about what inspires you—be creative with your thinking. For example, texture inspires me. When I go for a walk, I don't just focus on my arrival at some destination, I look for texture: the shapes of layered leaves on the ground, the silver and brown of bark on the trees, and the way filtered light lifts and defines bare branches. My aesthetic is delighted by the deep orange of a rusted metal sculpture in one yard and the striated patterns of a bamboo fence in another. Both the weathered gray sheen of concrete on the sidewalk and the layered clouds across the sky intrigue my senses. The opportunity to see, with an artist's eye, the color and forms of the world around you can serve to inspire if you pay attention to what your senses respond to. In the words of Leonardo da Vinci, "Develop your senses—especially learn how to see. Realize that everything connects to everything else."

Nurturing the daily aesthetic of our inner creative nature is a way to engage with life. The texture that invigorates my core influences my dress in layers of wool skirts with patterned leggings and worn leather boots. It is the basis for the aesthetic of our home in the paintings we hang, the woven blankets on the beds, and the colors in each room; it is why I work with my hands, attending to the physical and energetic layers of the body; it is how I approach writing, threading together words and stories. I make a practice of noticing and interacting with beauty in textural forms throughout each day. When we respond to the beauty around us, we weave this beauty into the fabric of living.

Tapping your creative currency feeds and fills your core energy with vibrance. This is the energy that gives color to your daily life.

Whether or not you make a living from these creative inspirations or pursuits directly, they refill the well within—the source for all you create and make in your life. The more your creative currency is flowing (because you intentionally dwell near this channel), the more abundant your inner creative wellspring will be, and the more you can draw upon it as a robust source.

You have found your creative currency when you are energized and inspired by particular ways of engaging yourself. For example, in my passion for writing I can easily lose myself for hours in the experience. I also find my spirit rejuvenated by this creative practice. But I'm not only rejuvenated; something happens in my energy field when I write. The energy in my center responds to the action of creative writing; it feeds my creative channel and aligns the creative field. Since writing is part of my creative currency, I make it a priority every day. Whether I spend fifteen minutes intentionally exercising my creative currency or carve out time for an extended session, I know exactly how important these simple tasks are to my overall creative life.

How do your access your creative channel?
What does your creative aesthetic respond to?

Let Go of Linear Pathways

Reclaiming your life as a wild creative involves letting go of linear pathways. Again, the old forms of shaping a career—a life—around monetary or achievement-oriented goals is the unbalanced masculine model that has dominated modern history, the results of which are negatively affecting people's mental, spiritual, and physical lives. In this "strive and drive" model, you might strive for a specific degree and profession, or you might plan your career path with a company by striving for a specific trajectory and then move into higher levels of responsibility and job stature. In the type of model where success is measured by the achievement of linear goals rather than by the health of the whole partnership, relationships can fall into a rut or a limited expression, such as one partner earning all of the income, or tasks and roles being defined by gender. Regardless of their focus, linear pathways leave little flexibility for the natural cycles of living.

Linear pathways might work when the economy is booming, but they are not reliable in a recession. Assuming a linear pathway ignores that economies (like life) move in ebbs and flows, ups and downs. During economic recession, college graduates with loans to pay off may find financial struggle and a profound setback to their dreams when their linear path fails to provide what was promised, despite all their hard work. Likewise, a person may follow a career path with a company only to be laid off unexpectedly when the company has a downturn, or may find that, in the ever-changing marketplace, their skills have become obsolete or outsourced. In the flow of life, a person can become ill, need to care for an ailing family member, or have a child who impacts their capacity to work or to fulfill other priorities. Relationships follow the cyclical flow of life as well, and learning to move with these cycles invites a greater capacity for true intimacy with oneself and others.

A linear pathway is rarely sustainable because, by its nature, it requires constant propulsion rather than more cyclical or natural patterns. The linear perspective, with its narrow definition of success, can lead to burnout or a sense of failure when goals are not met. In fact, it often fosters quiet desperation, because there is never enough—never enough money, or time, or status, or security. Instead of feeling wholly nourished, as happens when what has been done or made is just right, linear pathways convey messages of scarcity. A feeling of depletion always underlies the day-to-day reality of each impulse and action. In fact, the productive intensity of a linear model often arises from a base of insecurity.

This routine sense of incompletion inherent in linear models— the sense of not quite there and never quite enough—diminishes the ability to relax into joy or contentment. And though a person might declare that they want to enjoy their life, if their life structures and energy systems are built on linear models, they may find that this enjoyment is elusive or temporary—until they make a new energy structure to live from.

With changing family dynamics and new models for living, the linear path is less relevant. As various business, professional, and even monetary models transform around us, purely masculine or linear trajectory pathways are dissolving. Again, we can respond to this change by building holistic or feminine models. For every woman and man who desires to live a sustainable and soul-filled life, accessing their personal wild feminine is increasingly essential to doing the work of creating new forms and embodying these new modes of being.

This time of breakdown—and breakthrough—occurs as we realize that many of the monetary structures, relationship forms, and work models that have given shape to individuals' lives need to shift in order to make room for a fuller expression of our truest selves. Rather than a sign of failure, we can perceive the change as cyclical, where the end of any cycle always leads to new beginnings. This is a time of necessary evolution and potential. Many previously rigid forms, like gender expectations and business models, are evolving for the better.

In the past decade, while making an intimate study of the human body and its creative energies, I have seen the potential of feminine energy to repair imbalances in this system and create new models when we recognize and cultivate its presence. Taking breaks from your schedule, seeing an illness as an opportunity for retreat, or stepping out of roles at work or home that no longer satisfy you can make space to fundamentally change the way you are inhabiting your days. As more feminine energy is reclaimed—and with it, the connection to our inner fire—the masculine structures will transform. We will witness and create new masculine models as we develop these potentials and reinvent our daily lives.

How have linear models been helpful and/or challenging for you?
Where would you like to have new models for living?

Use Holistic Measures of Success

To move away from linear models, it helps to define new holistic measures of success. To review, a linear model requires visible achievement: *How many of the garden projects were accomplished? How much exercise did I do, or how far did I run? Have I read every self-help book on my shelf? Is the whole house immaculately clean? Have I taken care of everyone in my family? How high is my salary? How much money have I accumulated? Am I being praised or noticed?* This type of value or success will keep you trapped in the never-ending treadmill of doing.

Shifting to a more holistic and cyclical model allows you to value other aspects of living and redefine success: *How is my spirit? How has my sprit grown? Am I resting and enjoying myself equally to accomplishing tasks? Have I incorporated two exercises from my self-help books into my daily life? Am I living sustainably? How am I sharing my gifts and receiving nourishment? Am I earning money creatively? How am I valuing my money and tapping my creative abundance? Is my family working with me, or how can we better work as a team? Have I savored the beauty of my home and garden? What am I making, and is this how I want to spend my precious energy? Am I in touch with my dreams? Have I spent enough time in the wild? What can I be thankful for or celebrate today? How am I honoring my sacredness?*

The country of Bhutan has realized that the health of its environment and citizens requires the measure of more than the Gross National Product (GNP), which most countries use to quantify economic success based on the annual production of goods and services. Instead, Bhutan has defined its measure of development as Gross National Happiness (GNH). Bhutan's government officials have invested in the concept that beneficial progress happens when material and spiritual development occur side by side, complementing one another. There are four main areas of GNH: *sustainable development, preservation of cultural values, conservation of the natural environment,* and *good governance.* The Centre for Bhutan Studies & GNH Research further divides these four areas into nine general contributors to happiness: *physical, mental, and spiritual health, time balance, social and community vitality, cultural vitality, education, living standards, good governance,* and *ecological vitality.*[4] Imagine what it would mean to live in a country governed by these principles. Oregon governor John Kitzhaber traveled to Bhutan in 2013 to learn more about how these ideas might apply to shifting his state toward social and economic sustainability. We would all do well to assess the governance of our lives based on such concepts.

We can begin within ourselves to define new measures of success. The linear model can only perceive marked achievements, while a more sustainable model measures the value of the steps taken and the simple achievements: *being kind to oneself, becoming more aware, understanding the value of presence, savoring ease and replenishment for the workload.* The linear mind-set needs proof, or a walking-on-water type of miracle, while the holistic mind-set realizes that it is waking up to the small miracles—the rainbow stretched across the sky, the smile on your partner's face, the emerging sprouts in your garden, your ability to breathe more freely—that will mark true progress over time.

Bringing Creativity Back Into the Equation

Though creativity is an essential part of generating vital energy, it is frequently missing from the equation of how we build our lives. My early personal path was focused primarily on achievement and earning top grades. I selected high-level classes in high school, like advanced math and science, even though these classes stirred zero passion in me. I thought art and other creative pursuits squandered valuable time, even though I came alive when writing creatively. In a society based on production and the productive value of its citizens, making art or studying something without tangible value seems superfluous. I adopted the typical focus of many high-achieving students and steered toward achievement-oriented classes. However, in all those years of striving and achieving, I misplaced my desires; I never stopped to ask myself what I really wanted because it seemed irrelevant. I was "doing" what I was "supposed to," such as earning my value with high grades along the linear trajectory of school success, college degrees, and professional success—never mind that life is rarely a linear path, or that linear paths can become boring or even deadening over time.

While awareness continues to grow about the importance of the gestational, replenishing side of this equation, there continues to be significant cultural messaging about being productive and linking productivity to one's value. These messages are prevalent enough that my oldest son began asking what he might be able to do to make a living when he was about eight, though this expectation had never been raised for him at home. I tell him, *Stay connected to your center and your passions, and you will find your way to making a living and a life.*

Doing well in school can assist his opportunities, but I am now aware that his creative potential is the essential part of his developing a productive and soulful life. In response, our family culture emphasizes the importance of one's creative currency. Creative pursuits are nurtured in our home, led by the desire of each child and supported by classes and opportunities to engage; developing a connection to one's creative currency is highly valued in our family. Nothing is more precious than loving the life you make for yourself, and nothing is worse than making a life and trying to fit within its parameters as an afterthought.

Maintaining creative currency requires balancing joyful, replenishing feminine energy with action-oriented masculine energy, for both women and men. Again, masculine does not simply relate to the male gender; rather, the term *masculine* refers to a linear way of directing energy. When a masculine model is made in the absence of the feminine, it overemphasizes such linear trajectories as making good grades in school, applying to college, finishing a high-level degree, finding a high-paying job, and traveling onward and upward toward material success. Its inordinate emphasis on action and production drives down the value of feminine aspects of the creative process, stifling both genders in the process.

Fortunately, the wild feminine never ceases to call, and so many of us find ourselves changing tracks from a linear path to a more intuitive one. Life circumstances such as having a baby, changing or losing a job, moving to a new place, getting divorced, feeling burned out, or graduating from college and finding a lack of employment opportunities can be the nudge that motivates the rekindling of your original creative potential. Whether you seek a new direction because you feel tired and uninspired by how you are living, you want more access to joy in life, you are in the midst of profound change, or you desire to reawaken creative passions and dreams, reconnecting with the wild feminine and then restoring the true vibrant masculine will endlessly enrich your wild creative life.

Tuning In to Feminine Potential

The feminine is all around us. Marion Woodman, a Jungian analyst who has spent a lifetime studying the feminine, writes, "The Great Work that is beginning is the realization of the feminine as the bridge between God and humankind."[5] In my work as a physical therapist, I stumbled into the feminine by accident. As I helped women achieve physical alignment in the pelvic bowl, sometimes the energy in the room changed and expanded as if touched by the divine. By paying attention to this expanded energy field, I began to study how we could access this field—and the creative currency it contains—with intent.

I noticed that when I guided a woman's breath and awareness to the left side of her pelvis and left ovary, her whole energy field expanded. Comparing the reaction in the energy field by directed breath to the right versus the left of the body led me to Dr. Leonard Shlain and his book *The Alphabet versus the Goddess*. In elegant detail, Shlain describes how the left side of the brain controls the movement patterns on the right side of the body, regulating the written word, logic, and linear processes: the masculine realm that emphasizes *doing*. He contrasts this with how the right side of the brain controls the left side of the body, regulating images and nonlinear, holistic, and intuitive processes—with the feminine realm that emphasizes *being*. In Shlain's research of early Mediterranean civilization and the demise of the goddess, he proposes that perhaps the rise of the written word reinforced the left hemisphere skills and tendency toward production, compromising the right hemisphere and more feminine values.

Both women and men have this feminine image–based, intuitive place from which they can draw energy; in fact, this is where much of the real creative work begins. Even though our culture continues to emphasize productivity, when we intuitively or intentionally stop our doing long enough to make time for the dreamy and expansive energies of the feminine, it becomes a source for new inspiration. In today's rapidly changing work and social dynamics, everyone needs access to their full creative resources. Whether we are faced with a particular job challenge, a series of tasks, a need for guidance, or even more energy in a busy day, taking a moment to pause, reflect, inhale, and access the right brain–left body feminine connection will boost our immediate sense of well-being and vital energy. Even more, it is the way to receive the energy download for reconfiguring your day or reimagining an aspect of your life.

> *What can you receive or notice about the beauty around you right in this moment?*
> *How can you access more of this in your everyday life?*

Feminine–Masculine Alignment: Dream before Doing

Contrary to the more familiar production-focused model, a feminine–masculine alignment places equal emphasis on being or receiving as it does on making a visible creation. It values dreaming and holistic perspectives as much as doing, and is in fact a way of informing and guiding the doing. Rather than calling for continual output, this more natural model recognizes that we are meant to receive energy first and then build with that energy. We rest and restore ourselves, and then we move and create. We are an essential part of the creative process, just as vital as what we are making. As the feminine presence expands, by receiving feminine intuition and inspiration, the masculine is then energized to make new forms that reflect our cyclical and sacred creative nature.

The secret to designing our lives from the creative center is to re-establish our connection not only to the feminine but to feminine–masculine alignment. We must recognize where we forgo the feminine and overaccess the masculine mode of doing. We must honestly evaluate where we operate primarily on output and production, noting any tendencies to work until we are depleted, frustrated, exhausted, irritable, or even ill. And we need to recognize the point where we believe our sense of well-being depends on how much we accomplish or achieve rather than on an inner state of harmony. In the presence of the stress to produce continuously, the body tends to constrict, tensing muscles, which reduces our energy flow. Fortunately, by recognizing the effects of stress on well-being, we can consciously reverse the constriction pattern and instead replenish ourselves by intentionally receiving the feminine as breath, downtime, nourishment, and dream cultivation. Receiving from the feminine first and then taking action with the masculine, we follow a more fluid and long-term, sustainable inner flow pattern.

Rather than running your engines on high in the "strive and drive" model, using the feminine–masculine flow is like surfing an energy wave; I label this model as "flow and go." When feminine energy is moving, a person can receive this energy and let it build until the movement shifts into a more productive phase. Likewise, when the flow is minimal or nonexistent, it is time to halt and simply be or seek restoration. Following this pattern is ultimately just as productive as "strive and drive," but what is produced occurs cyclically and arises from a centered place. There may be a wealth of production and then a fallow phase. With feminine focus, however, what you make is more likely to be in alignment with your soul because it moves from your own energy center rather than from what the outer world dictates.

Each of us enters the womb on a tide of powerful and deeply creative feminine energy. Yet because we are rewarded for developing an externalized sense of value based on what we do instead of who we are, this early feminine connection is often forgotten. Again, it's important to remember that though the feminine is accessed in the female body, this feminine potential is not just related to women. As the mother of three sons, I have witnessed how essential the feminine is to their sustenance and joy. To give them access to the feminine, I create opportunities to engage this aspect of their energy fields. I take them to wild places, do simple rituals, say blessings, and encourage activities that help them tap into the dreamy feminine, whether it's playing guitar, drawing, dancing, taking pictures, making swords and shields with found materials, or even finding Zen-like calm by passing a football back and forth. Because boys often communicate in the non-verbal realm, I see them more clearly with my feminine awareness. In the presence of a vibrant feminine, their masculine energies are playful, inventive, and raw beauty in motion.

The Wild Feminine Potential for Men and the Masculine

Societal messages and rewards are studiously directed toward promoting "manly" behavior in boys and men, and offer shame and punishment to those who openly explore their softer feminine sides. Fortunately, when men are listening, they instinctively find their way to their replenishing wild feminine energy. The experience of our family friend Kevin illustrates this perfectly.

One night at dinner, we talked about the path one takes to find oneself. Kevin had attended Amherst College, perhaps following his father's academic road map. While he was partly at home in a university culture, he also found that the competitive debate and intellectual rigor bordered on combativeness, causing him to become overly defensive. Kevin's true learning began when he left college to work as a fisherman in Alaska; Alaska helped him rekindle the wild part of himself. He arrived in Bristol Bay with a small boat and fished for salmon. As he placed his nets, he felt the salmon brushing against his legs in the water, and there, in the inlets at the mouth of the Kvichak River, Kevin dropped out of the intellectual space and into the space of the body.

Living in relationship to the land, Kevin developed what he called his "perceptual processes." In contrast to his college life, which required a sharp mental focus that was often in relation to another person, Kevin contacted a deeper sense of self and a way of allowing himself to be in the wild. He honed his intuition, noting a new awareness that arose from the lower, more rooted aspect that comes from walking upon the land in relationship to its natural rhythms. He came to discover his inner realm and his instinct—the primitive sense that guided him in fishing or in responding to grizzly bears and all manner of the wild as he became a part of it.

Kevin began to recognize the senses of his emotional body and the intuition of his heart. He told me that while he was surrounded by the water and the wild, it felt safe for him to open up because he didn't have to protect himself from the intellectual repartee of his academic life. I noted the irony that the wild, with all of its potential perils, was the place of safety for him. We spoke of the expansiveness of self that can occur in the wild. For Kevin, the fluidity of the diurnal tidal rhythms of fishing created a corresponding fluidity in his state of being. He felt the boundaries between him and his surroundings were thinner there, and his dreams flowed like the water that surrounded him each night in his boat. Even after he left Alaska, Kevin would carry with him this expansive sense of his connection to all that was within and around him.

After Kevin's experience of being in the wild, no matter where he lived, he intentionally sought out places with broad vistas so he could look across the landscape and feel his expansive nature. When he returned to Alaska each season, he prepared himself before leaving home to realign with the wild. He "emptied" himself of expectations, fears, and apprehensions in order to "live right" and align with the natural flow he was about to enter. It was a process of giving himself over to whatever the journey would bring.

On the night of our conversation, Kevin had retired from two decades of fishing, but the imprint of his time spent among the salmon and the water is still evident in the way he lives and carries himself.

Ultimately, while people find feminine–masculine alignment when they are in relationship with their inner selves or nature (as Kevin learned), this can be further enhanced by the ways in which they step back into their life and into their dynamic partnerships with others. For example, I use my feminine nature as a source of inspiration to generate content for my books and website, but then work with members of a publishing team (both male and female) who use the masculine qualities of shaping a particular form to edit and produce the books on a specific timeline, and set up web links and worldwide distribution forums.

When people learn to recognize the feminine in their lives, most realize that they have long been able to enjoy the feminine state of being when they are "in the zone": while gardening, creating art, experiencing nature, or playing music or sports. But it is the intentional use of this capacity in both the feminine and masculine aspects of the energy field that makes the difference in their being able to creatively cultivate their whole life. In order for this work to go smoothly and the outer masculine expression to expand to its full potential, it's first important to know how to access the feminine capacity, or left energy field, for yourself.

Engaging the Mystery

There is great mystery in the beauty each one of us contains, yet in the midst of the daily grind, we can lose touch with it. A practice that restores our embodied sense of this potential within is an essential part of reviving the feminine field. Clients have said to me, "I want to have more connection to spirit or to the sacred, but I don't know how." My work is to show them that the connection to the inner sacred begins with accessing the feminine while offering tangible ways to do so.

On one level, it is a sensory awareness—a practice of noticing what can be invoked simply by being more consciously aware in the present moment. If, however, your sensations have been dulled for a time, it may take greater effort to come into contact with the breath and vibration of pure presence. Being near a birth or death—when spirit enters or leaves the body—brings an instant awareness of the essence of life and what matters to us. But mostly, we forget about the daily miracle of being alive. Taking a journey to a sacred site or traveling to a place of your dreams can reawaken your senses, and going into nature can heal your sensory system. Prayer, meditation, ritual, and healing practitioners can assist you. Remember that even if you have lost this sacred connection, it is still there within you, awaiting your active engagement.

Opening to the sacred by tuning in to the sense of awe that comes from feeling your connection to something greater restores the feminine–masculine current within. Start by noticing the breath of life in your own body. Notice the simple blessings in your day—an inner ease, a loved one's touch, a hummingbird in the yard, the blue-orange sky at dusk. When you notice, you become more aware of the beauty that is always there.

The feminine is nourished by experiences that allow sensory awareness to partake fully of any given moment, particularly in more experiential and less language-oriented ways. These could include taking a walk outdoors or engaging in another activity while using mindfulness (simply becoming more aware of present sensations). Even the simple practices of awareness in the moment and the receipt of the blessing that moment contains can repair and strengthen your connection to the feminine presence—your creative currency—that will nourish you.

Again, once a strong feminine current is flowing, we can use this feminine resource to develop new masculine patterns. The energy we allow ourselves to receive becomes the basis for our daily actions: parenting, homemaking, career building, earning a living, and building community. By transitioning from the masculine (linear) production model, which emphasizes putting energy outward, we can base life instead on the natural receptive qualities of the feminine, which guide and inspire us before we take action. In the presence of a robust feminine, each action itself becomes inspired and infused with divine potential. By discovering the feminine–masculine flow and the way one enhances the other, you can remake your daily rhythm and embody how you will give (masculine) expression to your (feminine) beauty—enriching your true wealth as well.

Exercise: Finding Your Creative Currency

Find a quiet place, a pen, and a pad of paper to do this exercise.

1. Take a moment to close your eyes and connect with the still point in the center of your body. Sense into this center—the physical/energetic interface of your creative field. Notice what is here for you. Are you tapping into or ignoring your creative potential? Are you in touch with this creative channel within or are you more focused on the outer world? Ask for creative insight from this inner space, such as *How can I better access my creative flow?*

2. Imagine the scene when you last felt vividly alive. Notice how this aliveness feels in your body and energy field. How does your creative-energy field look and feel?

3. Now open your eyes and make a list of the activities that inspire your passion and creative flow. Write for at least ten minutes, or until you complete a list of ways to generate creative currency.
4. Review your list and make note of how often you are engaging these passions. Circle three items from your list that stand out and make a commitment to adding them into your routine (at least weekly).

Notice how the activities on your list can be linked to bringing more energy and abundance into your life. For example: add more movement or exercise to your day, bring your camera to work, take an art class and create gifts for others, frame art or favorite family photos for your home, wear more color, or spend time outside. Notice the shifts in your energy and the experiences that arise from cultivating tangible creative currency.

Bring Your Passion to Life

We hear the phrase "follow your passion" in terms of work, but this does not mean you need to make a living from it; rather, it means your living will benefit from the infusion of your passion. Steve Jobs explored a range of topics while enrolled at Reed College, and though he didn't continue in academia, he discovered a passion for calligraphy. When he began to design computers, his experiences with calligraphy inspired him to build typeface options into the computer interface. The simple addition of typography introduced the first creative aesthetic to the computer and was made possible by his bringing his passion to his work. Creating work infused with passion is the essential ingredient for meaningful success.

When my husband, Dan, and I were just out of college and trying to formulate our careers, we could have used this advice to intersect passion with cultivating a profession. While sorting out our working lives, we alternated between two extremes: following pure passion (such as for the environment) toward careers that did not directly make use of it (like graduate-level science) or dropping passion in favor of more practical pursuits (like attending medical school). I studied biology at the University of California at Berkeley, and first considered pursuing an advanced degree in ecology. The problem was that, though I loved being in the natural world, studying the environment through a scientific lens was uninspiring to me. I was good at science and it came naturally to me, but applying science to my experience of nature was passionless for me. In hindsight, I now see that true scientists are motivated from within and are passionate about understanding the natural world in a scientific manner.

The nearest I came to sensing passion in my science education was while studying quantum physics and medical anthropology, which examined such things as the multilayered potential of the universe and healing in native medicine. Right there would have been a sign pointing me toward my future had I known what to look for. The energy work that I am blessed to do now has much in common with the esoteric principles of energy, light, and matter that make up quantum physics. It also reflects a deep understanding of the energy of the body that many ancient medicine systems contain. There are always clues about what makes us come to life and who we are meant to be if we are paying attention; these clues are the markers for making our way in a manner that both inspires and provides.

Before I understood how to read these clues, I briefly entertained the idea of becoming a medical doctor. Fortunately, through hands-on mentoring I came to a more complete understanding of what actually fueled my passion and what diminished it. While shadowing one of my anatomy teaching assistants on her medical rounds (she was pursuing a dual degree in medicine and public health), I realized that the hospital setting itself, the complex illnesses of patients, and the difficult procedures that took place there gave me a leaden feeling in my body. When the TA had to draw fluid from the lung of a gravely ill patient and made multiple attempts to insert a long needle into his back, I had to leave the room to keep from fainting. Outside in the hallway, recovering my breath, I knew that this was not the career for me. The abstract notion of being a doctor appealed to my sense of achievement—and at this point in my life, achievement was my primary measure of success—yet the reality of daily life as a doctor felt dreary.

Meanwhile, Dan's undergraduate degree in business led to his first job in corporate banking. However, he was uninspired by his job; his tasks held no relevance for him. While environmental work was a more direct passion for him than business, he wasn't sure how to follow his passion into financially viable work. After entering a graduate business program to develop entrepreneurial skills but still not knowing how to combine business and passion, he found a volunteer project with Pacific Rivers Council, a river and native-fish protection group in Eugene, Oregon. That project turned into its own organization, which he eventually led: Salmon-Safe, an independent eco-labeling program that works with farmers and urban landowners to inspire land management practices that help restore watersheds.

By bringing his passion for the environment to his business field, Dan made a career for himself that blended a variety of his talents and interests. Over the years, he has received hundreds of resumés from graduates of environmental studies programs who are challenged to find work because, as job seekers, they have an abundance of passion but little applicable skill. It was Dan's business skills that allowed him to make use of his eco-passion, a perfect illustration of balancing masculine and feminine energies to enhance creative capacity.

The Gift of Your Beating Heart

The ability to follow your passion requires that you be able to listen to the inner workings of your being and track your heart's desire. But your heart's desire must be of equal or more importance than the messages from the outer world in order for it to be reflected in your life. To track this for yourself, ask these questions: Does your work inspire you? Does your life include ample room for creative expression? Have you stayed in contact with your dreams for yourself and allowed these dreams to evolve? Are your intimate relationships nourishing and reflective of who you are? Can you share your gifts with the community? Are you in touch with the passions of your heart and soul? The gift of your beating heart and its impulses is that it will lead you toward—rather than away from—the channel that feeds your core essence.

In my early twenties, working in a science lab revealed how deadening the pursut of a degree in graduate-level science would be for me. I could barely tolerate the eight-hour days I spent doing lab work. But if environmental science was not my path, then I thought I should perhaps re-examine medical school as an option. I reasoned to myself that maybe I could enjoy being a doctor in a small office. At the end of each work day in the lab, I walked home. On my way, I passed a small medical office with a few doctors and a pediatrician. One day I decided to go in. The office was quiet. I spoke with the receptionist and asked if the pediatrician might have time to talk with me about her experience in medicine. To my surprise, the doctor had a moment to spare and sat down in the empty waiting room to answer my questions.

I asked her: "How do you like being a doctor? How is it on a daily basis?"

She responded with a question, "Do you love medicine?"

"I'm not really sure," I replied, "but I know that I want to have children, and whatever I do has to work with being a mother."

This was the answer that came to me; this was the answer of my heart. She peered into my eyes and spoke from her heart too. "My husband and I married young. We made it through undergraduate school, and we made it through medical school. We even made it through my residency. But then, after I had finished all of my medical training, we realized we didn't know each other anymore. There wasn't any room for a life during all that time, and we lost touch along the way. We're in the process of a divorce."

That was all she needed to say. "Thank you for being so honest," I answered gratefully. To me, it was a clear message.

How many careers do people work toward only to lose touch with what matters to them? If we are only in touch with our achievement—regardless of whether that achievement relates to school success, professional success, job security, income level, or one's sense of inner worth—the work life we make will be out of touch and out of sync with the desires of the heart and soul. The achievement-oriented careers (that are typically perceived as models of success) such as medicine, law, or doctoral study require such extended periods of striving that there is rarely room to ponder one's full life. Life is put on hold while the striving continues toward a particular goal—until the training is finished, the degree is achieved, the job is secure, the equity position or salary is realized. By the time that pinnacle is reached, one's life, body, relationships, and dreams may be worn thin or long lost.

Here is another story that illustrates how lost we have become in our career trajectories: I was talking with a young doctor about the intensity of medical residencies, and he shared his personal experience. He was completely exhausted during a day of his residency after many nights of interrupted sleep and patient care. While observing a heart surgery, he was asked to hold the patient's heart. He took the heart in his hands while the surgeons worked—and fell asleep while holding this heart. *He fell asleep while holding someone's beating heart.* Shocking, isn't it? Yet many people expend immense effort on making a living while asleep in the moment, without access to what truly matters for them.

As a self-defined striver accustomed to linear pathways, when I found myself with no plans for graduate or medical school, I felt disoriented. The other idea I had been exploring—becoming a physical therapist—did not directly interest me; at least, not in the way I had seen it practiced when I sprained my ankle and the physical therapist gave me a prescribed sheet of exercises. But there was something that drew me toward it. Though my rational mind could not understand it, I felt my being stir and move in that direction—the guidance of the feminine that I had not yet learned to recognize. Even in my early days of shadowing other physical therapists, I felt more at home; they were social and active. The people in my science-lab group toiled for long hours and worked right through holidays without so much as a nod of cheer; and they scorned going out of their way to celebrate a colleague's birthday or promotion. The physical therapists had potlucks, took vacations, helped people, and seemed to enjoy what they did.

In the end, I followed my intuitive impulse toward physical therapy and later found how my passions for bodywork, women's health, ancient medicine, energy, and writing could come alive in this profession. I brought my passion to my work, and the work unfolded into a bright career in response.

Likewise, my healthcare practice reveals an increasingly widespread desire to recalibrate back toward that which inspires and makes us come alive. I see clients of all ages and phases of life, yet a common theme echoes among them. Here are some examples of what they write as personal goals on the intake form: *to get in touch with who I am; to feel more passionate; to discover my intuition; to remember my dreams; to deepen my understanding of the feminine; to create new ways of being; to be more whole; to reinvigorate my partnership; to feel sexy and radiant; to know what to do with my life; to bring my true self into my work; to change what I am doing; to make my dreams come true the way I see others making their dreams come true; to know what I have to offer; to hear the language of my body; to believe that I am creative and to be able to discover that creativity within; to reach new levels; to live from a place of strength and confidence rather than a place of fear; to be the person I know I can be.*

Everywhere you find someone making a vibrant career path, an amazing product, a beautiful creation, a love-filled relationship, or a bountiful life, you can be sure that it is somehow linked to their passion and the creative flow that arises in the midst of engaging that passion. Remember the gift of your beating heart; be wide awake and fully present in order to make use of it.

TWO

The Energetics of Creativity

The privilege of a lifetime is being who you are.

—Joseph Campbell

Don Elijio, a Belizean shaman who mentored one of my teachers, was worried about the health of his community because the women were dreaming less. Before he died at the age of 103, he told my teacher, Rosita Arvigo, that dreams were a place to receive guidance from the spirit realm; they connected to the ancient wisdom of the body, particularly the womb. Yet in the course of the many decades he worked as a healer, he noted that women were having fewer and fewer dreams. And community life was guided by the dreams of the women, so if they were not dreaming, this guidance was less available. He felt perhaps this inability to dream signaled a lack of attunement with the deeper currents of life and the essential connection to spirit.

Don Elijio told Rosita that the people of his village used to gather near the fire in the morning to hear the dreams of the menstruating women because they contained essential wisdom and psychic information for the tribe. When I tell this story to modern women, who have typically experienced shaming around their menstrual cycle, they are shocked by the thought of the community gathering for this purpose.

Though some might dismiss this notion as outmoded or superstitious folk medicine, the story represents knowledge from a time that was less ruled by the intellect and more connected to the natural world. Don Elijio was not only referring to the ability to dream but to the energy current that connects to a greater field of awareness through dreams.

Even in our modern lives, our dreams—not just the dreams we have at night but the dreams that manifest as the passions we desire to orient our lives around—have tremendous relevance for staying in touch with our soul and wild nature. Remembering how to dream, even while wide awake, allows us to live from the clarity and resources contained in our own creative-energy field. When we dream, we move beyond perceived limitations into the greater realm of spirit and our own connection to the spirit place.

What dreams or passions have you put on hold?
What energy does this contain for you or reflect about your true self?
How might you bring this energy current into your present-day life?

Become a Creative Generator

We are born creative beings. That is, by moving the energy of breath and the divine through our bodies, we are meant to create—homes, families, careers, communities, and daily expressions of ourselves and what we are bringing to the world. Great creative luminaries like Steve Jobs, Oprah Winfrey, Eve Ensler, Bob Dylan, and countless more "cultural creatives" (an altruistic, spiritual, and socially progressive segment of Western society), change makers, musicians, artists, activists, and entrepreneurs are consciously using this big-vision capacity to direct their lives to their fullest potential. Of course, it is also possible to live as fully with a lower profile; it just depends on an individual's vision and what each individual finds at their center. In any case, these creatives are generating energy and making connections that enable their true expression in the world. When you know your full creative capacity, you, too, can become a creative generator and live from the abundance of this place.

The Divine Energy Field

Many spiritual teachers relay the concept of unity—the notion that "we are all one." In terms of energy, this relates to the divine energy field that connects all life. When we are feeling expansive, we are likely connecting to this greater field and the life force it contains. When we lived closer to the wild, we moved in sync with this broader field. Much of our modern lifestyle does us a disservice by taking us away from and even disrupting this natural connection; so it is even more essential to know how to cultivate it for ourselves. Creative generators, rather than perceiving themselves as separate, tend to unite with and draw from the expanded capacity of the divine creative field.

Play: Do You Access the Creative Field?

Many creative generators are in tune with imaginative play in the creative field. But many of us internalize the message prevalent among high achievers that work is more essential than play or open time, whether we're pursuing education or a career. People sitting in the library studying when their peers are out socializing and relaxing are universally approved of as the ones who are making "good" use of their time. Only in recent years have technology startups in Silicon Valley helped show that the best creative ideas arise out of free-form associations and unstructured play. Still, while children spend much of their time in the imaginative realm of play, as they grow to adulthood, they frequently lose touch with this potential. Pablo Picasso said, "All children are artists. The problem is how to remain an artist once he grows up."

Being able to play may require remembering how to play. When I first tried to play with my children, I noticed my awkwardness in free-form play. The problem was that my overdeveloped cognition, honed through years of school, had forgotten how to exist in the spontaneity that play entails. To move through my own resistance to play, I had to just be in the awkwardness of feeling unsure how to do something that is natural but often lost. Being with the uncertainty while trying to play with my children, I sometimes heard an inner voice: *This is silly—you are wasting your time.* But in allowing the voice to fade and staying with the intention to play, something shifted, and a very silly and spontaneous part of me arose in the spaciousness.

Now, when I am able to lose myself in playfulness, whether with my children or just as a way of engaging the world, I observe the dreamy quality that arises—where anything is possible. This is how to access a personal connection to the energy field of creativity; it's how inventors and visionaries maintain their awareness. The inventions of electric light, flight, automobiles, television, cameras, space travel, computers, the internet, and other countless flashes of insight that have become businesses or breakthroughs all arose from this plane of imagination where children play. As adults, we would do well to return there and dream our full potential, leaving the critical and practical voices behind, to see what we can create from this place. So, find the children, pets, or playful friends in your life and remember how to tap into the energy of play that offers direct access to your creative field.

How do you like to play or access the creative field?
What could you do more of that would invite the energy of play into your day?

Desire: Where Are You Going?

Desire relates to your energy flow within the creative field, and it is essential for generating creative currency. In the same manner that play is relegated to childhood, staying in touch with the desires that fuel your dreams can be challenging when you are navigating a school or career path, or any outer trajectory that reinforces achievement based on a map others have made. Ponder your connection to desire with these questions: Do you know what you want for yourself? Can you shape your day based on what you desire? Desire directs energy; and when you are clear about your desires, you are more precise in your creative aim. When you know what you want, you can have better boundaries around how you choose to spend your time.

Danielle LaPorte, an author and well-known blogger, created a multimedia program called "The Desire Map" to aid the process of identifying "core desired feelings" as the first step in being creatively productive. LaPorte asks the question "How do you want to feel?" And she suggests that rather than making to-do lists or setting goals, we identify how we want to feel in the various aspects of our lives, allowing these core desired feelings to guide what we do. LaPorte says, "Knowing how you actually want to feel is the most potent form of clarity that you can have. And generating those feelings is the most powerfully creative thing that you can do with your life."[6] Rekindling your relationship with desire is another means of drawing from the creative channel that will sustain you.

> *How do you want to feel on a daily basis? In your personal life? In your professional direction?*
>
> *How does contemplating these desires shift your creative direction or commitment to dreams?*

Focus: Where Is Your Attention?

Once you are clear on what inspires you and what you desire for your creative self, then your creativity needs regular focus on those areas. Your weekly schedule can be built around these key places to provide the creative practice to hone and develop whatever you are making.

I do this in my life by organizing my schedule into focused blocks of time. I allocate two days each week for scheduling clients in my health practice so that, on those days, I can deeply focus on my creative work as a healer. Then I also schedule two three-hour blocks for creative writing, and at least one three-hour session of creative visioning for my business. I find that those uninterrupted blocks of time are essential for settling fully into the creative flow. In the same manner, I do most of this work during the hours that my children are in school, so that I can focus on mothering my kids when they are at home. And I am ruthless about pruning away superfluous projects or activities; I routinely prioritize two to three primary creative vocations: healing, writing, and mothering. During a focused period of writing, for example, I do nothing but write. I leave the dishes in the sink and the bills on the table, and close down my WiFi on my computer to prevent common distractions. I do not answer the phone, fold the laundry, surf the web, or address anything but what I have chosen to attend to for a period of two to three hours. This routine focus ensures that my creations receive the benefit of directed attention over time. This careful tending of my creativity in specific directions offers a deepening of the creative experience and sharpens my skills in these areas, allowing my experience with a particular creation to evolve.

There is power in practice. If you are just starting out, it can take time to build up your concentration stamina. Even if your schedule is crammed, finding a half hour a day to engage in the activity you love will result in actual creation and the natural improvements that come over time. Creative energy/currency is one of your most valuable assets. Make certain that your creative priorities (as intentionally chosen by you) are prominent in your weekly schedule, with regular access to your field of inspiration, and that these priorities are producing your desired feelings—so that you can generate the energy and the creative currency for your life.

Exercise: Simple Creative Checklist

Find a quiet place, a pad of paper, and a pen to complete these questions:

- Do you have routine solitude and time to connect with your center and creative passions?
- Are you inspired?
- Is there ample opportunity for play or access to the creative field in your life?
- Are you clear on what you desire to experience or create?
- Is your routine focus in alignment with your inspirations and desires?
- Are you exercising your creative capacity and building your creative currency?

If all answers are yes, press on. If you have any hesitations or have answered no, address the issues until the answer is solidly "Yes!"

Identifying Internal versus External Value

Creative generators distinguish themselves by recognizing and empowering their potential. Internally, they recognize their own value; and in being creative, they are simply giving expression to this value. They don't make the mistakes that keep many people from generating their full energy potential; they don't try to justify their value through work or by creating products. Examples are the employee who constantly overworks herself to prove her worth and the volunteer who gives tirelessly without regard for his own needs. This external type of valuation is conditionally dependent on one's level of productivity. And more truthfully, it masks a common fear that we are not valuable or worthy just by ourselves, apart from the identity of outward accomplishments.

Many artists have to face this valuation process in themselves, either choosing to follow the creative inspiration within (which may or may not translate into outer material success or recognition) or trying to direct their art toward what others perceive as valuable. Neither way is right or wrong, but individuals who understand their own value will have an easier time following creative passions just for the inherent growth, enjoyment, and journey they offer.

The essential component of allowing your own star to shine and experiencing the creative energy of your field is to claim your value as incontrovertible. Rather than establishing value through work (and striving for validation), it is infinitely more powerful and creatively freeing to acknowledge your value and then bring it to the world. Rather than being defined by what you create, bring who you are to what you do. You are the star.

Energy Session: Redefining the Meaning of Value

Stella came to my office for an energy session because she was feeling burned out. She'd had an early and successful corporate career that she left to tend first one and then a second child. Now that her children were entering school, and in the absence of the intensive caregiving duties of the infant and toddler periods, Stella began taking on several independent work projects. She did not need the additional income but missed the energy that her corporate job provided. She found herself working at all hours of the night to fulfill her obligations on these various projects, along with tending to a home and the needs of her school-aged children. Her husband had a demanding career as a surgeon, and all of the home duties fell to her.

I invited Stella to bring attention to her creative center in the pelvic bowl. As soon as she focused there, she felt cold and empty. There was no energy. She was busy attending to so many projects that she had little time to nourish or even connect with herself. The projects (and parenting tasks) were running all of her energy channels, and her energy was dissipated. Now that she was focusing on her center, she could see how all these projects drained her. I asked her to sense why she was intensely engaging in these various work projects, especially when they were giving little in return. Stella listened to her body and then said, "I realize that I feel like I won't exist if these outer projects die away. It's as if they give meaning and visibility to who I am and a part of me that is not expressed in the home as a mother."

I helped Stella see that if she could connect first with her intrinsic value, her creative impulses and the way she directed her energy and time could arise from that place rather than from a need to affirm her value. Instead of navigating by seeking validation, she could navigate by what excited or invigorated her. In this way, she would be free to redirect her creative energy in the manner of her choosing, and her homemaking alone might feel more fulfilling. Or she might direct her creative expression to a new arena that inspired her. Her current work projects reminded her of her past life and the authority she commanded in the corporate world, but because her sense of internal value was not intact, she had to seek project after project to feel energized, unaware that she was continuously filling a void.

For Stella, the first step toward nurturing her creative flow was returning to her center and establishing her inner and true value by being more present with herself. In our session, as she focused on the energy of her center, she felt sadness. Long ago, she had loved to hike and dance, make festive meals with friends, and cultivate her garden. She looked at the compressed pattern of her current life from this inner clarity. She was always rushing along: rushing kids to school, and then hurrying home to do laundry and begin her work projects. She worked as long as possible, then squeezed in school volunteer work. She rushed the kids home from school and to their activities, raced through dinner and homework, and hurriedly put the kids to bed. After they were tucked in, she set up her computer again to resume her work projects. Her life looked like a frantic race. Stella felt a squeezed sensation in her body that mirrored her daily energy usage. She asked aloud, "What is the hurry—where am I racing to?" She had no time to savor the blessings of her life, no time for pleasure or deviation from her never-ending project list. Her energy system was still operating on linear models.

To change the energy patterns that define our lives, we must look directly at them. Though it was difficult to witness how she was spending her energy, Stella was already reclaiming more of her creative power by consciously observing her own pattern. It was up to her to decide which patterns to keep and which ones to change by choosing how she would like to focus her creative energy. She responded that she wanted to give expression to her creativity from a place of inspiration rather than one of need. Instead of feeling compelled to work and managing by default, she wanted to know what fueled her creative essence.

I invited Stella to release the energy of attachment to these various projects, letting go of them in her mind's eye. She imagined each one moving with her breath away from her body and down toward the earth. With this release of the energy attachment to her work, I invited her to let go of the linear energy model as well. Once she had completed this release, I guided her to return to her center and bring all of her creative energy with her. There, in the quiet center, Stella felt lighter and more free than she could remember. She saw more clearly the daily patterns that weren't working for her and where she might redesign her life. Illuminating Stella's center with this focused meditation reflected to her an intrinsic value beyond her ability to be productive in the professional realm.

Next, I invited Stella to fill this clear, creative space with her own desires. She immediately made an intention to cultivate spaciousness in her life for enjoying the fruits of her labor. Shifting from the previous sense of compression within to a pattern of spaciousness could reform Stella's outer energy pattern and the way she managed her daily schedule. Stella also decided to choose one inspirational creative pursuit as a routine focus for her creative outlet. This was the recipe for Stella to hone a creative essence that receives as much or more energy than it gives, and to develop a natural creative model as a basis for living.

Navigate Your Creative-Energy Field

In developing the practice of Holistic Pelvic Care bodywork that I now teach to other providers, I created a method to work with creative-energy patterns and navigate the creative field as a mode of healing. The process of restoring pelvic vitality requires realigning the core creative-energy patterns. And in helping women replenish their core health, I discovered a highly effective tool: you can generate your own creative currency by learning how to navigate your personal creative field—how to *read* the flow and *realign* the field as needed.

The art of bodywork comes from knowing which patterns in the body are dysfunctional (in order to change them) while also enhancing the beneficial patterns. The art of energy work is similar but requires an acute awareness of the subtle patterns of energy, in order to address alignment and flow.

During a treatment session, I work with clients by applying my energy field and awareness to sensing densities, blockages, or constrictions in their energy as well as their overall pattern of vibrancy. Then I work with them to guide their ability to sense this within themselves. My goal is to empower others to work with their own creative energy centers. With each client, I begin by teaching sensory awareness—the ability to sense what is happening in the energy by feeling the subtle sensations in a particular place that I guide awareness to.

After I teach a client to sense the core pattern, we increase alignment with three tools that can shift energy: *inner vision* (visualizing), *inner sensation* (sensing), and *breath* (sending energy using breath). The body–energy field may provide insights during a session through images, words, realizations, or guidance that helps to align the center. I find it endlessly fascinating. The client stories I share in this book are composites created to reflect the healing potential I have witnessed in my practice. Though Holistic Pelvic Care combines hands-on physical and energetic techniques, these stories include the purely energetic aspect of this work and the insights that are relevant to working with your own creative-energy field. Again, this applies to both women and men, since we all gestate and form our body–energy field in the pelvic bowl and then make our own inner map from this information.

The linear aspects of living may tend to take us out of the center of ourselves, yet whenever I sit with a client's core energy, I find myself right at the heart of matters. I have found that the measure of a person's relationship to passion, dreams, and desires often reflects how much they are able to connect with and navigate their creative-energy field—and coming home to this field will bring you back in touch with these aspects as well.

How to Map and Use Your Unique Creative Field

In my healthcare practice, I receive information about a person's creative field by observing their body language and energy flow as they talk about their creative joys and challenges. Core vitality and pelvic health both relate to feeling creative. In women, the patterns within the body—and particularly the creative center of the pelvic bowl—affect how they channel their creative energy, whether they are conscious of this or not. Bringing these patterns to consciousness is the first step in redefining core patterns in beneficial ways.

This creative field containing the body–energy interface applies to men as well, because, again, we all gestate in the female body. Both women and men have a creative field (the field of energy that influences the flow of life energy) that relates to this early gestational space. And a person's relationship to their creative nature is often entwined with family attitudes toward creativity. Patterns imprinted in the creative field become patterns of living and creating.

We inherit many of these patterns from our lineage and life experiences, but we can interact with and reshape them in ways that better serve our creative abundance. In working with the energy fields of both men and women, I have found it helpful to identify and map patterns in the creative field. Noting supportive versus restrictive patterns, and then realigning these core patterns enhances creative potential. When alignment and flow are present in the core creative map, a person will feel increased creativity and notice that life is more readily aligning with the creative dreams they have for themselves.

The Body's Creative-Energy Field

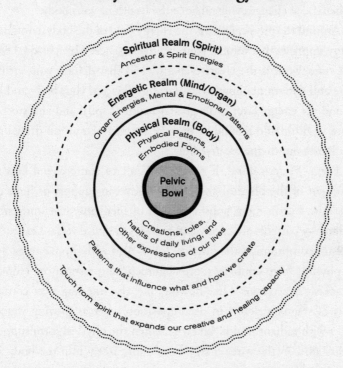

This model for the creative-energy field illustrates the physical, energetic, and spiritual dimensions of the creative center. The physical body, including the pelvic bowl and creative organs, contains both the physical patterns and embodied forms that define your creative capacity. The physical patterns relate as well to the physical structure of your life: your work, your relationships, the daily habits that organize your time, and how well these core structures are made to dwell near the creative channel of your life. These core forms can be supportive or disruptive, but they can also be changed to better align with the creative field as you learn to embody more of this potential range within and around yourself. Sometimes physical symptoms in the body can be a sign that the structure of your life is hindering optimal flow, and making beneficial changes will enhance the health of your body.

Around the physical core is the energy field of the body, containing energy imprints that inform your creative essence. This personal energetic framework is the creative-energy field that defines your creative range and determines how creative energy flows in your body and life. Beyond the energy layer is the greater realm of spirit and ancestor: the mystery within and around us that we are part of and can draw upon to enhance our divine creative flow.

For a Western mind, it can be difficult to comprehend how the alignment of the physical and energy body can support or limit creative flow, but in more holistic models of medicine, it is understood that energy patterns affect physical patterns and vice versa. Less energy presence compromises the physical form. And with more energy flow, the physical form contains more alignment and resonance. Think of a brackish river versus a free-flowing one: the standing river contains pools of stagnant debris in decomposition whereas moving water is bright with radiant health. Likewise, when the physical form supports vibrant flow in the core, energy flows more freely into the body and the outer life. Creative currency, as core energy flow, is essential for health, wealth, and making structures that build on creative currency to increase this abundance.

In my work, I was initially surprised, but I came to profoundly understand that messages about creativity and its potential are deeply encoded in our bodies. And this inner framework defines how energy moves through us and into our lives. Even more, we can interact with these encoded messages in order to strengthen the beneficial ones and reshape those that limit creative expression and growth. In fact, a key to reclaiming creative potential is to work with the alignment within your center. We tend to think of the patterns in our bodies and lives as permanent forms, but each—from our deepest cells to the vastness of our creative capacity—is a dynamic expression that can evolve and change. Working with your personal creative field can be an endless source of inspiration.

Exercise: Exploring Your Creative-Energy Field

Use this meditation exercise to connect with your center and inner wild creative landscape, the interface of your creative energy and body. Find a quiet place, a pad of paper, and a pen to begin:

1. Sit in a comfortable position. Bring awareness to the center of your body, particularly the lower aspect of your core that connects with the earth. Notice your pelvic bowl, this powerful creative center, and how it connects to your legs and feet to touch the earth. The lower body brings spirit down to the tangible forms of our lives. Ponder your own spirit–body interface for a moment: what is its shape or color in your mind's eye? Take the pad of paper and draw what you see or sense. Then set the paper down and continue the exercise.

2. Now practice ways to connect with and align the energy of your own field. First, use your sensory awareness to become familiar with the different sensations in your physical body and the energy layer as well. Where do you feel warmth? Where does it feel cool or even cold? Where is there a sense of energy or vibration of aliveness? Where does it feel stagnant or dull? Are there specific sensations you notice while scanning your body and energy field, like spaciousness, tingling, tension, fluidity, or compression? When you focus on the sensations, notice that they begin to change. Keep focusing and they will change again. In this way, you are using your sensory awareness to work with the energy in your own field.

3. Sensory awareness is helpful for two aspects of energy medicine: increasing your connection or presence in the body–energy field, and working with places of blockage or stagnation. Try sensing into part of your field that has less vibrance or energy; spend a few minutes there, and the energy or vibration will increase. Now notice a

place of blockage that may feel like tension or compression; sense into it and the constriction will change or release.

4. Beyond sensing, try the second way of working with your body–energy interface: focused breathing. Send a directed breath; that is, breathe toward an area of your body or energy field that has less vibrance. Notice what changes as you do so. Repeat the directed breath but toward an area of flow this time, and see what happens. Observe how your breath moves and supports the overall energy.

5. Now add the third way of working with the body–energy interface: visualizing light or colors along with your breath. This adds another dimension to working with your energy. Using your inner vision, you may receive an image or insight from your creative field visualization. Some people are more adept at either sensing or using inner vision; notice what works best for you.

6. After using sensing, directed breath, and inner vision to connect with your creative field, take a moment to give thanks for this creative potential within your own center. This is a sacred place—like a medicine wheel within for communing with spirit, receiving guidance, and giving form to your creative dreams. Now take the pad and draw this spirit–body space again. Notice what has changed from the initial drawing.

After you learn to sense your creative-energy field, the next step is to cultivate alignment in this field so that energy flows effortlessly through its framework and into our lives. Once the core patterns of the body are aligned, we can better interface with the greater spiritual realm, which contains the energy potential of the universe. Great creations come from this place, and great creators know how to expand into this broad field to bring spirit energy into form. When we are creative, we are working at this interface of spirit and body for ourselves. (See the "Attuning Your Energy–Body Interface" exercise on page 44.)

*Are you feeling a connection with your center and a flow in your life?
How is the alignment of body, energy, and spirit in your creative center?
Where in your life would you like to channel more creative flow and
receive more creative currency?*

Our Original Creative Imprint

Let's further explore how our creative fields carry an imprint from our experience of gestation in our mother's body and creative field. Think of the time in your mother's body as the beginning of your creative foundation. The eggs in your mother's ovaries were fully formed when she was a fetus in her mother's womb. So the egg that you arose from was wholly intact in your mother's ovary when she was in her mother's body, thus transmitting the coding from two women. Likewise, you were an egg in one of your mother's ovaries (either the left side or the right side) her whole life—until this egg traveled down the fallopian tube and became the basis for your body.

Each one of us spends decades imprinting experiences about life and creativity—that we have no conscious memory of—in an ovary on either the left or right side of our mother's energy field. I joke that different personalities correlate with a "left ovary" or "right ovary" way of being. In actuality there is some truth to this, because each side of the body does correspond to half of the energy field (and brain sphere). Though these unconscious imprints are sometimes associated with negative traits, imprinted potentials also serve as your creative assets both from your connection to your mother's body and from her mothering. In this regard, our creative fields have multiple layers and dimensions of information that we can work with to enhance our own creativity. Whether you're male or female, becoming aware of your personal wild creative landscape and mapping the energy field in yourself allows you to engage or reshape this original foundation to restore access to a whole new creative range.

Attune the Energy–Body Interface

The physical nature of the universe, from bodies to homes and daily habits, gives form to our lives. Every morning, I sit with a cup of tea, looking out my window. I watch the light spreading across the sky and the day beginning on the street below. The sensation of the warm teacup, the moment of stillness observing the view from my window, and the quiet of a city slowly awakening are the forms that make up my morning ritual. In fact, this beginning is such an integral part of my routine that I feel something is missing when I do not have this reflective teatime to start my day.

Consider your typical morning and day. What habits, structures, and routines give form to your life? Remember that it is your body through which your creative energy moves. The habits of living, the company you keep, and even the thoughts you have on a routine basis become the forms of your life. Yet you have a choice in how you use these forms, and you can change those that no longer serve you. Think about where you could add some creative time, such as early in the morning before anyone else is awake, during a lunch break, or at the end of the day. Ponder the following questions:

When are your two most creative or reflective periods of the day?
What are you currently doing with those times?
Is that what you want to be doing or would you like to change your daily habits to better tap into this creative potential?

Forms such as the simple tea ritual I described support and nurture creativity and the presence of spirit as a routine. Anything that contributes to allowing you clear creative space, time for contemplation, an open and curious mind, insightful thoughts, and encounters with thoughtful people will bring more creative energy and opportunity for conscious creativity. In the same way, harmful behaviors, cluttered space, heaviness in the mind or heart, and hurtful relationships will diminish and discourage these aspects. To maximize creative potential, you need forms that nourish spirit.

Creative activity begins as an energy—an inspiration in one's center—and invites you to give it a form, a body. This is a way in which energy moves from the universal chi (energy) field into our bodies to give us life. We can work with this inner flow by being creative. Even taking a walk with the intention of invoking wonder, or seeing the world through new and open eyes, is distinctly different from walking to a specific destination. Try taking a walk with the focused intention of arriving somewhere, and notice what happens in your body. Then take another walk with an open sense of time or place, simply noticing what you encounter along the way. Observe the difference in your body. The second way of walking leaves more room for the energy of spirit to inspire—to connect—with the energy around you.

Take note of your spirit–body interface. This relationship and communication between spirit and body is vital to the creative process. Just as too much emphasis on the physical realms or focused intention may cause a lack of inspiration or even a feeling of stagnation in the body, there can be too much emphasis on spirit or energy. When in the midst of creative inspiration and full of spirit, many artists or creatives travel too far into this realm and forgo the physical needs of their own form. They may become out of touch with their body and ignore their bodily needs for rest or food.

If I have been writing for too long, spending time dreaming in the spirit realm but not tending to the basic physical needs of my body or home, I will begin to feel an imbalance in my center. To restore my connection to the physical realm, I may take my dog for a walk, put on music and dance, or even do the dishes. Likewise, spending too much time in the tasks of work or in getting things done without giving sustenance to the spirit can lead to stagnation and feeling uninspired. As in life, there is a balance required between spirit and body for optimal creation. When there is balance, spirit gives life to the body and the body gives form to spirit.

Exercise: Attuning Your Energy–Body Interface

Use this meditation exercise to attune your inner wild creative landscape, the interface of your creative energy and body. Find a quiet place, a pad of paper, and a pen to begin:

1. Sit in a comfortable position. Bring focus to your center. Connect to the inner spaciousness with your sense awareness, breath, and inner vision.

2. Move your awareness through your body, noticing the sensations as you do so. Notice the boundaries of your body by traveling around your perimeter. Feel this house of your spirit.

3. Now sense the energy of your body as a pulsing warmth within your body. (There is also an energy flowing through and around.) When you sense your body's energy, it is typically more diffuse than when you sense its physical aspects. Energy has the quality of light and is less defined than your body's physical boundaries. Notice the sensation and movement of energy. Sense and notice how it interfaces with your body.

4. Bring awareness to the left side of your body. This is typically the right brain–left field feminine aspect of your energy (although it is reversed in some people). It relates to the less linear, more fluidly creative aspect of your energy. Notice the sensations on the left side of your energy field. Send a breath directly to your left aspect and lean into this space. Ask your left side how it is best engaged: how can you more readily access its energy? See if any images or activities come to mind; if so, take note of what they are. If none arise, make a point of bringing more awareness to this left side of yourself to strengthen the connection with your more intuitive aspect of *being*.

5. Bring awareness to the right side of your body. This is typically the left brain–right field masculine aspect of your energy (although it is reversed in some people). It relates to the more tangible and form-based creative aspect of your energy. Notice the sensations on the right side of your energy field. Send a breath directly to your right aspect and lean into this space. Ask your right side how it is best engaged: how can you more readily access its energy? See if any images or activities come to mind; if so, take note of what they are. If none arise, make a point of bringing more awareness to this right side of yourself to strengthen the connection with your more direction-oriented aspect of *doing*.

6. Bring awareness back to the sensations in your core body–energy interface after contacting both the left and right hemispheres of your energy field. Notice what has changed: perhaps you have greater awareness, more flow, a sense of warmth or pulsation, or you feel peaceful or quietly engaged.

7. Now imagine bringing energy in from the outer ring of the creative field and realm of spirit, like taking a full breath of energy. Receive from this vast reservoir for your own energy field. Draw in nourishment, inspiration, abundance, deep connection—whatever you are yearning for. Remember that you are part of this greater creative field and can activate your divine potential. Take this activation back into your daily life. Make it a practice to move from your creative center and whole-field vibrancy.

Tended versus Disrupted Energy Fields

The energy field can be tended by honoring the earth and one another, but it can also be disrupted by trauma and stress. You can observe this in your own body: when you feel love and connection to the flow of life, you may feel more at ease or open in your center. Likewise, when you are stressed or angry, the body tenses and you likely feel closed off from others and the natural flow within. If you examine a piece of land near a highway or disrupted area, any plants there are likely to be stressed or growing poorly; and you will likely experience stress while standing there because your body feels the disruption. Compare this to a place in nature where the wild is intact: there is a quiet aliveness running through it all that you will feel in your body and energy field as well.

The rapid pace, linear modeling, and distance from the wild in modern life tend to disrupt the energy field around you. Restoring the creative flow in your center, dwelling near the flow, and then tending your creative energy will realign this field. Notice what you may have been doing, even that which is equated with a "successful life," that may be disrupting your field. Learn to recognize how it feels when tended. Evaluate work, daily habits, relationships, time in the wild, spiritual practice, care of the home and body, creative expression, patterns of thinking, and ways of being. Make two lists: *What disrupts my field? What tends my field?* Move toward the tended field—your creative field is worth cultivating with care.

Body Language and the Creative Field

I recently came across an effective illustration of the way the body gives expression to the creative field in an interview with of one of my favorite business creatives, Marie Forleo. Forleo was speaking with Mastin Kipp, a web-based entrepreneur and creator of a popular blog *The Daily Love*. Watching Marie's interview, I was struck by Mastin's body language, particularly as he relayed a story about a crucial conversation with his mother.

Mastin described beginning to follow his soul's calling, which was leading him away from his previous life constructs and toward his "daily love" blog of insights and quotes. In a series of life-changing events, he lost his company, his lease ended, and he and his girlfriend broke up. Rather than being discouraged by this run of luck, Mastin chose to see it as a "divine moment." Free now to devote his full attention to *The Daily Love*, he moved into a friend's closet-sized pool house to save on rent. At one point, Mastin didn't even have internet service—even though he was running a web-based company—and relied instead on free WiFi in the neighborhood. His well-meaning mom asked her twenty-eight-year-old son when he was planning to find a paying job. Mastin said it was painful to hear this question from his mother in the midst of discovering something far more important than a job—the faith and courage to pursue his dreams.

After several difficult conversations with his parents, Mastin was finally honest about the change in his life direction. As he shared the part of the story about expectations for making a living that no longer matched his inner guidance, I noticed that he gestured to the right side of his body with his hands, as if pointing toward a path from his right hand that he was no longer following. In my clients, I have seen that the right side of the body and energy field tends to map more of the linear pathways and common ways of being in the world, including more masculine pursuits like following a traditional career path.

Mastin continued, "I'm going here now . . . I am doing *The Daily Love* . . . I'm called to it." And just as I have seen countless times in my office when clients speak of their hopes and dreams, as he said these words, Mastin simultaneously pointed to the left side of his body and energy field—toward the path of his dreams. The left energy field tends to relay the feminine realm of pure inspiration. At the close of the interview, Mastin stated that he has intentionally made space for feminine receptivity in his business practice.[7]

Envisioning Your Inner Creative Map

Imagine your energy fields mapped to register the right-side masculine and the left-side feminine as distinct from one another. The left side of intuition and holistic perspectives is where our dreams and hopes reside; we must engage with this part of our energy field to make contact with our dreams. The right side of the energy field, which provides strategic direction and the ability to accomplish tasks, is essential for bringing inspiration into a tangible form. To be able to generate your creativity as well as manifest your dreams, you first have to understand how to access both the left and right hemispheres of your energy map to tap into the whole creative field.

In my holistic physical therapy practice, I became interested in the subtle patterns that organize our energy. As clients have shared their stories with me, I have seen that challenges in the pelvic bowl often relate to creative challenges in their lives, and that the medicine for these difficulties lies within as well.

The way that you inhabit your body reflects how you inhabit your greater creative field. If you only inhabit the linear, more production-oriented aspect of the creative field, you will focus on only one side of your energy flow, missing out on compelling intuitive insights and inspirations. You may become so busy "doing" and keeping up with your work and life obligations that you forgo your essential purpose of giving expression to the soul. Yet if you only access the dreamy and inspirational aspects of your energy field, you miss the strategic focus that will give form to your dreams.

As I saw in the video of Mastin sharing his story, when I observe clients telling their stories and expressing their frustrations, I notice patterns in body language that reflect a common creative pattern: again, the linear or logical aspects of life (masculine traits) are mapped on the right side of the body and energy field, while the more dreamy and creative aspects (the feminine) are mapped on the left side of the body and energy field. This means that as people talk about the practical aspects of their lives, such as taking care of the family, working in their professions, or getting things done in a practical manner, they gesture with their hands to the right side of the body (which corresponds to the left side of the brain). Likewise, when they talk about more fluid and timeless tasks like imagining their ideal day, sharing their inspirations, expressing gratitude and love, or relaying their personal dreams, they gesture to the left side of the body (which corresponds to the right side of the brain).

Of course, we need both aspects of our energy field to be creative and fulfilled: the feminine aspect that receives inspiration and the masculine aspect to give it structure. The challenge is that too many of us disowned the feminine aspects of ourselves in childhood because sensitivity is not valued or is even discouraged and mocked in our culture. The feminine includes the home and our earliest relationship with our mother and the female body. Unless someone actively carves out space to honor the feminine, it can be easily dismissed. Developing a habit of acknowledging the roles and effects of the feminine can help preserve respect for it. For example, I talk with my sons about the courage it takes to be vulnerable and express feelings. Respect for the feminine also relates to respect for the female body, so I talk with them about menstruation and the sacred nature of the blood that lines the uterus and feeds our first hint of a body after conception. In this way, I want them to know the power and beauty of the feminine as an imprint that vibrates in their earliest cells. Similarly, I encourage them to explore their creative feminine aspects.

Depending on family code, some children may be discouraged from expressing the feminine traits of nurturance, sensitivity, emotional expression, dressing up, dancing, flamboyance or visible creativity, and so on. Male children particularly find themselves struggling in a world that insists they be strong, stoic, and heroic—minimizing expression of all emotions but anger and distancing themselves from the feminine nurturance of their mother. From outright suppression and attacks on a child's feminine nature to more subtle levels of shaming, these messages continue beyond the family to include teachers, the broader community, and the increasingly influential and pervasive media. Though these messages to turn away from feminine expression can also be intended to protect children from teasing, they further add to a child's sense that something is wrong with inhabiting the feminine aspects of themselves.

They reinforce the false notion that the feminine is weak, when in truth, it is a powerful energy current. Another truth is that in order to give children more room for full expression, we have to return to the places where we abandoned the feminine within ourselves.

After childhood, becoming a member of society and making a productive life can lead to the false conclusion that the feminine (or creative passion) is extraneous. But feminine pursuits—homemaking, gardening, mothering, nurturing, holistic living, being creative or artistic, remaining sensitive and tuned in, emphasizing being rather than doing, making things by hand—are only perceived as nonproductive if the primary measure of productivity is monetary or status based. Clearly, making money and achieving status do not equate to happiness or a sense of inner peace, yet many people form a life based upon the pursuit of security or wealth without regard for the needs of their feminine (or inner) nature. If we stayed in contact with what inspires the feminine and directed our outer life based on remaining connected with this core inspiration instead, our lives would be both more soul filled and more expressive of the soul.

Exercise: Reworking Your Map for Creative Flow

What we pay attention to grows in our lives. If we focus on stress and what is not going well, we tend to amplify its presence. If we emphasize our intended creative directions and the abundance that develops in the midst of creative flow, we amplify this as well. Choose more of what you want in your life by mapping new directions for your creative focus. Find a quiet place, a pad of paper, and a pen to map your creative flow.

1. Make a list of what supports your creative flow. Write for as long as is necessary to capture any ideas that come to mind.
2. Now reflect on your general habits. List the primary focus of your efforts and daily patterns. For example, are you focusing on work,

stress, caregiving? Does your day include any self-care, play, and/or creative expression? List whatever comes to mind.

3. Examine what you need to change in order to experience more creativity, as well as any habits that might be stifling creativity or overemphasizing production. This can involve changes to energy or structural changes to your schedule. For example, if unscheduled time enhances your creative flow, give yourself permission to add some openings in your week.

4. Return to the list and circle your top three sources of support for creative flow. Think about how to incorporate these forms of support into daily habits in order to increase the routine experience of creative expression, shifting any unhelpful habits you recorded on your second list. For example, instead of having something to eat (when you may be actually seeking inner fulfillment), take a moment to do a mindful meditation. Instead of absentmindedly surfing the web when you need a break from the tasks at hand, take a quick walk around the block or soak in the sun to re-energize yourself. Rather than continuously forging ahead on your to-do list, prioritize simple ways to refocus your energy on being, such as relaxing back into the present moment and noticing the beauty it contains.

5. For the next few weeks, intentionally move toward your creativity-supporting habits. Many of us tend to focus on the challenges, stresses, and work of each week rather than the joys, pleasures, and creative impulses that will increase with our attention. Make sure that your primary energy and focus are where you mean for them to be. In this way, you make a new framework to support creative living.

By being intentional with your daily use of creative energy, you redraw the map that your energy follows. Creative intentions and practices become new energy pathways that are strengthened with use. Tend to your creative energy for the wealth that it is, and you'll discover more abundance for yourself—and ultimately have more to share with others.

Expand Your Creative Reach

There are moments of pure potential in our lives when we are in such a flow that we feel and contain more of what is possible. This might happen during a simple moment of gardening that makes a broader connection to the powerful energy field of the earth. It can be a moment of parenting, when inhabiting the field of unconditional love. We may find it working through a challenge or difficulty and reaching a point of new ground. Witnessing the sacred in a simple act of gratitude or a profound ritual broadens who we are to become one with the divine. Birthing a child, being present at a birth, or tending to someone who is dying also brings us into contact with a sacred expansiveness. In each of these examples, contact is made with the realm of spirit where unformed potential resides. But it does not start with this lofty goal; more often than not, the commonality across these encounters that expands your creative reach is the intention to be of service.

To build tangible forms from your creative dreams, you need inspiration (the idea), passion (the energy to make it happen), and then service (the purpose of your creative direction). Being of service to the divine creative flow brings this high-frequency potential to the world; and when you are acting in centered, whole-creative-field service, the world will receive it. If you are doing something creative—working on a project, seeking a partnership, sharing your vision—but do not feel fully received, it may be that you are still expecting the world to reflect or reveal your value rather than knowing your value and bringing it to the world.

The first step remains knowing your value—having a visceral understanding of the unique presence of your soul. From this place of value, match who you are with what the world needs. Matching the potential of your soul to a particular need in the world expands your creative energy to the whole creative field.

Where do you place your value, or how would you like to reclaim this placement?

What is the unique energy of your soul?

How will you share your value with the world or connect with the broader creative field?

Understanding the Meaning of Service

There is a difference between service that depletes you or is driven by a need for validation and service that fills you up. Rather than "helping" with your service, which tends to assume that others are not capable of helping themselves, true service is more of an equal sharing. To be in service does not mean that you do not receive something in return. In fact, when you match your core inspirations to the needs of your community, you discover a way of being in service that is replenishing.

For example, I volunteer at my children's school when I feel a core inspiration in my center to do so; I don't volunteer from a place of guilt or because a particular task needs to be done. In this way, my own energy capacity is part of any decision to offer my service and may be more or less available at a particular time, depending on the state of my energy. Likewise, my offerings as a teacher, mother, and friend tend to be related to my gifts as an energy reader or writer, so my core inspiration is reflected in the act of service. In this way, even as I give of myself, I am also nourished—by spirit, by the response of another, by knowing my part in the community, by the joy of sharing my divinity. Service that reflects your core inspirations and your potential (rather than seeking to affirm your potential) provides untold benefits for your creative field.

I offer service in my work as a healer, assisting clients in taking better care of themselves and recovering more of their creative range.

Nothing gives me greater joy than teaching someone how to discover the power and energy medicine right in their center. This work allows me to share my gifts and receive a bountiful practice that supports my family and my ability to be present in tending my family. I give and receive from a place of service, and the abundance is exponential. However, once again, I monitor my own well-being as a part of this service. I work a part-time schedule and receive care from my own holistic healers in order to replenish myself each week. Even as we do the good work in giving of ourselves, we need clear boundaries for when and how to do this; we give our best forms of service when operating from a full and robust energy field.

Before we can be of service from a place of core inspiration, we must be in touch with our passionate zest for life. The quality of our passion reflects the overall state of our connection to the feminine. Besides lacking the potential for service, a life made without tangible connection to the feminine as a wellspring of creativity is one that is prone to burnout; masculine productivity without feminine fire is a hollow shell. The feminine is fuel and guidance for the masculine and has the capacity to generate limitless inspiration for every aspect and stage of life.

If you feel burned out in any way, it is time to set down your masculine productivity and return to the feminine aspects of yourself. Make your first act of service one of rekindling your feminine fire. Stop doing and just be for a time; reacquaint yourself with this feminine nourishment within. It may require that you remember lost aspects of your desires or expressions. Once you rediscover what inspires your feminine, follow its direction. See where it leads. Notice what stops the inspiration and reorient toward what nurtures it. Return to a mode of doing only when your feminine presence is bright and strong enough to light the way.

What inspires your feminine essence?
What masculine forms are you making?

Which aspect of you is in need of more tending or new forms of expression?

Energy Session: Retooling for Feminine Inspiration

John came for an energy session while going through the motions of life but not feeling deeply connected to it. In describing his history, John mentioned that his mother was emotionally distant and had suffered from depression throughout his childhood. I could sense in John's energy field that his focus was on the external aspects of his field rather than the place of creative wealth in his center. Asking John about his creativity, I learned that his main day-to-day activities included working out and performing a job with an investment firm that provided a good paycheck but did not really inspire him. Male or female, whenever a client tells me they are uninspired, I typically find they have lost touch with their feminine place of inspiration. Also, since our first connection to the feminine is from our mother, if she is not present in that space, it can initially diminish our ability to connect there.

I asked John when he had last felt inspired. He thought of something, and his energy field brightened as he recalled a camping trip deep in the woods with his dad and brother when he was about twelve years old. I asked when he had last been hiking or out in nature, and he could not remember. His daily routine rarely strayed from working and going to the gym. Though it may seem obvious that just moving through the daily grind might not offer much access to passion, the focus on professional success often causes people to lose sight of their inner needs or dreams simply because they become accustomed to certain habits; they do not perceive what they are missing.

I invited John to think of his center as a place of rich potential and resources and asked if he would invest in spending time there. Coming into his center was like entering a foreign landscape, possibly because it had been so long since he had been in relationship with his internal realm. In John's case, having a mother who could not nourish this core place in him made it more likely that he would miss the value that it held and seek connection elsewhere. Focusing on his center, John recognized that when he came home from work, he turned on the television or surfed the internet. Imagining himself sitting at his computer, John said, "Watching myself just looking at a screen, I see what a waste of my time it is. I don't even remember what I look at on the computer, and yet I spend time there when I could be outside or doing something else." He reflected on his work and realized that much of his daily focus was on solving problems and building assets for others rather than on anything that had to do with himself or his desires. Recognizing the habits that take us away from ourselves is essential for deconstructing these patterns and making new choices and patterns that better serve us.

As John focused on his own center and moved through the layers that kept him disconnected, such as his job and screen time, a beautiful radiance emerged. He began to breathe more fully and to settle into the expanse of his own energy. I made a comment about this beauty that was arising from his own center, and he opened his eyes. "I don't think I've ever heard the word beautiful in reference to myself," he said. I had reflected a truth to him that males rarely receive—this validation of their own beauty—yet it is the source of creative potential for all beings, male or female. The main task is to rekindle this inner radiance, realizing that it rightfully belongs to each one of us and that we have a choice in how to use it.

John suddenly recalled a friend of his who had been asking him to co-rent a woodworking space where they could exchange tools and spend time on projects. John had been too busy to even entertain the idea, but now he realized how much he wanted to work with his hands and connect with his friend. He decided to make it a priority and to start listening to what he wanted to do rather than what he thought he had to do, replacing screen time and excessive work commitments with running in the park or being outside. Returning to the center of his being was the place to begin restoring a solid presence in the center of his life. This shift was sure to bring a physical and emotional return on his energetic investment.

To create a life of meaning, make a conscious intention for the direction and focus of your creative energy. A good measure of this is to ask these questions: *How would I like to be spending my time and living my life? Does that differ from how it looks right now?* If the answer reflects how you are already living, you are on the right track. If not, redirect your creative energy toward the way you want to live and utilize your life essence. You are a bright star, and your creative energy is meant to give expression to this radiance. What inspires your brilliance? Navigate by the passion of your own creative-energy field, and remember your dreams that bring this energy to life. The world (and you) need, the illumination of your light.

THREE

Honing Your Creative Edge

Today, like every other day, we wake up empty and frightened.
Don't open the door to the study and begin reading. Take down
a musical instrument. Let the beauty we love be what we do.

—RUMI

Creativity takes courage.

—HENRI MATISSE

As a dance and theater professor on the East Coast, my sister works to engage and inspire creativity in her students. On the first day of class, she takes a survey, asking them this question: Are you creative? Initially, about 10 to 15 percent of the class perceive themselves as creative. A short time later, at the end of the semester, after students have explored the essence of creativity not as a specific form but as an ability to be expressive, she repeats the question. The effect of reframing their preconceived concepts of creativity is measurable; an overwhelming majority of these same students now see themselves as creative.

A great barrier to creativity is your own perception that you are not creative. Feeling uncreative limits the creative current. And shame is often hiding beneath the feeling of not being creative. Children, early on, express themselves spontaneously, drawing, moving, laughing, and touching from a place of creative impulse. But when a child receives the message that their impulses are wrong—the drawing does not look like anything, the voice is off key, the movement is not precise enough, the note is not right, the sound is too loud—shame enters the picture. Whether big or small, shame stops creativity in its tracks. Even in childhood, artistic talent and creativity are paired as equals; creative gifts are weighted by burdensome expectations. Or, alternatively, if children get the message that they aren't inherently creative, they will often retreat from creativity to avoid feeling shame.

In my health practice working with women and the pelvic bowl, I am intimately familiar with shame. Most women carry shame about the female body, whether from early associations, body-image issues, gender, femininity, menstruation, sexuality, or self-expression. In fact, shame often defines the relationship a woman has with her body, and it limits access to the creative potential within. But the important lesson about shame that I have learned in my work with women is that while it is a layer that dulls creative potential, it does not damage the latent potential within.

Shame plays a profound role in men's access to their creativity as well. Having sons, I see how creativity can be dampened in males because they desire (and the "male code" often require them) to be seen as strong and powerful. If boys (or men) do not feel successful in early attempts at a skill or an activity, they often avoid it rather than endure the discomfort and vulnerability they feel in revealing that they are not yet good at something. Any place or time that men deviate from the male code (enforced by women as often as men) of strength, power, and invincibility by admitting vulnerability, being imperfect at a task, or showing emotion, they are often met with shame from others.

Internalized shame equally affects men and women. People can still be creative when they have not addressed their shame, but its expression will be limited. By being willing to delve into your center, going toward instead of away from shame, you can triumphantly reclaim the whole creative field. The key is to recognize the shame as a layer separate from yourself. Separating the sense of shame from what it is attached to allows you to retrieve these lost aspects of your creative expression and discover their applications in your present life.

Address Shame to Reclaim Creative Range

Though most of us avoid shame and anything connected to it at all costs, we must address shame in order to reclaim lost aspects of creative and general expression. By being willing to identify those aspects of our creative expression associated with shame, we also discover places to expand our creative range.

Dr. Brené Brown is a research professor in social work and a leader in the field of shame and vulnerability. In one of her key discoveries that arose from her research about shame, Brown found that the resistance to feeling or revealing our vulnerability actually holds us back from our potential. In an acclaimed TED talk about her research, "The Power of Vulnerability," she relays her findings: "Vulnerability is the core of shame and fear and our struggle for worthiness, but . . . also the birth-place place of joy, of creativity, of belonging, of love." We may avoid vulnerability in order to numb difficult feelings, but Brown reveals that in doing so, we limit our capacity for "connection, living wholeheart-edly, being seen, innovation, creativity, and change."[8]

Brown was surprised to discover that people she categorized in her studies as living "wholeheartedly" allowed themselves to be vulnera-ble. Since she was having difficulty with vulnerability herself, this led Brown to a personal crisis and breakthrough point. She began exam-ining shame and vulnerability, and working with them in her own life. The catch is that people are generally uncomfortable with feelings and topics related to shame and vulnerability. In fact, though Brown had more than six million views of her first groundbreaking TED talk and received many subsequent invitations to speak, the business venues interested in her work asked that she avoid any references to shame or vulnerability, instead focusing on "innovation, creativity, and change." Brown responded to this notion in a second TED talk, "Listening to Shame." She says, "To create is to make something that has never existed before; there is nothing more vulnerable than that."[9] In other words, if companies want creative employees, they must recognize the benefits of vulnerability and address issues of shame in order to foster innovation. To succeed requires the willingness to fail and perhaps the willingness to experience the vulnerability that either failure or success can bring.

Brown has continued to focus on these challenging topics even though they produce discomfort in many people, because the results of her research have struck a profound chord. She was inspired to continue her exploration by this Theodore Roosevelt quote that she includes in her second TED talk and follow-up book, *Daring Greatly*:

> It is not the critic who counts; not the man who points out how the strong man stumbles, or where the doer of deeds could have done them better. The credit belongs to the man who is actually in the arena, whose face is marred by dust and sweat and blood; who strives valiantly; who errs, who comes short again and again, because there is no effort without error and shortcoming; but who does actually strive to do the deeds; who knows great enthusiasms, the great devotions; who spends himself in a worthy cause; who, at the best, knows in the end the triumph of high achievement; and who, at the worst, if he fails, at least fails while daring greatly . . .[10]

In her second TED talk, Brown speaks to the general temptation to "stand outside the arena" (of life) and only "go in there when . . . bulletproof and . . . perfect." But she goes on to say that we never reach that point of bulletproof perfection and that, even if we could, "that is not what we want to see; we want you to go in . . . and we just want . . . to dare greatly." According to Brown, "Vulnerability is our most accurate measurement of courage," meaning that having the courage to "dare greatly" requires being comfortable with vulnerability (even in the face of shame that says "You are never good enough" and "Who do you think you are?"). Brown explains that while both men and women experience shame in a similar way, what causes the shame often differs by gender. For women, shame says to do it all and do it perfectly, and conveys a web of unattainable conflicting expectations. For men, shame is more focused: do not be perceived as weak (which means exhibiting basically any feminine characteristic). Brown suggests that cultivating comfort with our vulnerability, regardless of gender, is the path to overcoming these restrictions that limit living by our whole nature.

Associations with shame have caused many people to give up creative aspects of themselves. They may have a creative impulse buried beneath internal messages of shame, such as *I'm not creative*, *What I have to say isn't that important*, *I'm not successful enough to be creative*, or *Nothing I create has any meaning*. Or a generalized sense of shame such as *I'm not worthy* can squelch any creative spark. Identifying and acknowledging shame are the first steps to liberating the creative energy beneath it. As Brown states, "Shame requires secrecy, silence, and judgment."[11] To reduce the power of shame in our lives, we need to identify it, talk about it, and bring empathy.

Beyond Shame to Presence and Expression

Shame is only a layer—one that often hides our greatest assets. In my healthcare practice, I have noticed that when my clients are willing to connect with the pelvic bowl (even though it brings up a sense of shame) and stay present with and move through the sensations of shame, they recover what is beneath it: a potent creative reservoir. In terms of expression, allowing a creative impulse to move your body or sing a song—even in the face of shame—can similarly enable you to recover your original creative essence. Refusing to be stopped by the appearance of shame is the way to reclaim your full creative range.

Knowing what I do about shame has kept me on the lookout for opportunities to foster creative energy in my children and counter their self-criticism or tendency to internalize shame. When school began it was particularly challenging, because children measure themselves against their peers. My youngest son entered kindergarten and made an expressive self-portrait that our family loved, but his peers teased him because the head was square instead of round. Never mind that the angular shape gave the portrait character; it became a limitation in his eyes after he heard the judgment of his classmates. His brothers and I kept at him, though, refusing to allow him to give up his creative ground to shame by encouraging him to see the beauty in the drawing. His oldest brother posted the picture on Instagram and then conveyed the results to his brother (from his peer-based account): twelve people liked it and posted many positive comments. It was a teaching moment for our kindergartener, the first of many lessons about how peers are not always right and to whom he should give authority.

Though I do cherish my children's creations and encourage them to feel proud of them, I also emphasize that their process of creative expression excites me even more than what they create. In being creative, if the focus is on a particular outcome, the creative energy can be constricted by the pressure to create something valuable. If the focus is on creative flow, however, then the expression and final creation is infused with that flow. For many of us, the early lessons about creativity emphasized the value (or lack of value) of what we created rather than the creative process itself.

Likewise, any expansion in your creative range—such as taking more time to care for yourself, making your creativity a priority, becoming more visible, finishing a creative project, asking for additional support, or otherwise stepping into new aspects of expression—may release feelings of shame. If you notice the sudden appearance of an internal feeling or scripting (*Who do you think you are? Why would anyone want what you have to offer? Who would help you? Why do you get to shine?* and so on), first recognize that the appearance of shame is actually a sign that you are changing your creative range and stepping into new or previously lost creative territory. Second, identify with your new direction, or shift your focus to the expanded movement of creative energy (rather than the sense of shame). Think of shame as a boundary that is no longer relevant. Finally, make a practice of connecting with the creative current or process and see how it carries you beyond the boundaries defined by shame.

Exercise: Expanding Your Creative Range

Find a quiet place, a pad of paper, and some colored felt-tip pens or markers.

1. Make a list of the various forms of creative expression you can imagine: taking photos, writing, dancing, singing, speaking in front of others, saying something unexpected or outside of your comfort zone, gardening, cooking, drawing, expressing your style, creating a new look, decorating your home, playing music, sewing, crafting, painting or making a work of art, viewing an art show or museum, sharing a new idea at work, designing a new aspect of business, making a playlist, crafting a story or a poem, telling a story, doing improvisation, playing with your kids, having an adventure, trying a new sport, taking a drama class, moving your body in a new way, working on intimacy with your partner, or whatever else comes to mind.

2. Circle in yellow the types of creative expression you've listed that make you feel uncomfortable or stretch your creative boundaries. Then circle in red anything that is associated with a negative feeling, such as shame. After this, circle your places of strength and ease in green. Ponder the patterns that shape your creative range.

3. Now look at the bridges you can make between places of ease and those of discomfort or shame. For example, if you feel awkward at social gatherings but at ease when dancing in your own home, try moving your body to music prior to socializing, to free your creative essence. The creative energy that you access with ease can assist your

places of challenge and clear shame, allowing you to reclaim valuable aspects of your creative range.

4. Identify as many bridges as possible to leverage your strengths and use them to expand your creative potential. Identify three key areas associated with shame (or other challenges) that you would like to reclaim; make a plan for doing so. For example, if you want to reclaim your voice, make journaling a daily habit; write a series of poems and do a reading for family or friends (or just read them out loud yourself); work with a counselor; express more of your feelings; start singing; or do whatever creatively inspires you to reclaim your voice. Give yourself permission and the means to embody the full range of your creative field.

Creative Blocks: What to Do When You Feel Stuck

In addition to a sense of shame, the feeling of being creatively blocked is another sign that there is creative range to reclaim. Though we tend to avoid areas in which we experience creative challenges or difficulties, they can contain valuable creative resources. In working with the body, I have found the hidden value in restrictions and blocks to overall alignment and flow. Restoring vitality and alignment in the pelvic bowl requires working with creative-energy blocks.

Just as our physical health is greatly helped by addressing places of inner stagnation or blockage, the creative current in our lives has a similar response of increased potential for flow. In a river, altering or removing the physical placement of rocks changes its channel and flow. The body acts like a riverbed for the energy flow, defining its overall range; so changes in the body or physical realm will change this range. In the river, the flow of water pushes rocks and moves debris, effectively changing the landscape as well. In the same way, we can address restrictions to creative energy in order to influence the creative channel.

Common creative blocks include not feeling creative, having many ideas but no structure for actually manifesting these impulses into reality, a sense of not being worthy or capable of creating dreams, or wanting to be creative but having no idea or form for doing so. In all of these barriers to creativity, there is important information to uncover; the barriers themselves contain the answers for transforming the blocked energy into creative flow.

Rather than removing creative blocks or only perceiving them as obstacles to remove, it is by working with them that we gain a deeper understanding of what they contain. Even in our lives, we may run into unexpected blocks—an illness that takes us out of work for a time, traffic that slows our pace, a project that does not receive the desired response. If we take the time to deepen and work with the block that is inviting us to move differently, we will receive something in the process: a gift of more insight, energy gathering, new possibilities or directions, an alternative perspective.

In the process of living and being creative, obstacles are part of the journey, requiring focus and, if we're paying attention, clues about what lies in store. Obstacles may occur near regions of untapped resources. When you know how to identify and address them, each creative block you engage will potentially restore more access to your creativity. These blocks can have roots in imprints from our lineage or the day-to-day messaging we received about creativity from our families, including what defines creativity and how it is meant to be expressed. While it may seem like a chore to take on your obstacles, when you find the keys to untapped creative potential, it is like discovering treasure.

The next section offers several examples of creative blocks and their potential to inspire your quest for new creative ground.

Lack of Inspiration versus Rediscovering Pleasure

Living with a poverty of inspiration dampens creativity. If you have spent years in school or cultivating a career, your energy and daily life have been shaped by the demands of your classes or profession rather than by a place within you. Or your family of origin may have dismissed creative pursuits as frivolous, discouraging your own creative development unless you had a particular talent. As a result, like a muscle that is atrophied, your creative aspects can be diminished by disuse or underdeveloped because they were never accessed.

The place to begin when you are totally out of touch with creative potential is to restore a connection with your senses. This can be as simple as giving yourself one daily dose of pure pleasure: call a friend, take a bath, make a treat, go to a favorite restaurant, visit a new part of town. Do something each day that arises from pure enjoyment, and reawaken your capacity for pleasure. And if you experience pent-up feelings when reconnecting to your inner expression or a long-lost sense of desire, this typically resolves as you more fully nurture yourself and respond to your sense of pleasure.

What will you savor today?
How can you act from a place of enjoyment or bring more daily pleasure into your life?

Distracted Attention versus a Quiet Space

Creativity can require quiet and focus, and these qualities are rather elusive in today's full-time-access multimedia world. The pure busyness and pursuit of linear tasks can block creative flow. To be creative means that you have to establish clear boundaries around your creative time and limit other distractions, like surfing the web, watching television, or even visiting with friends. It can even be a hunger for the creative essence that causes you to seek entertainment, excess food, or empty pleasures. But until you know and address the source of your hunger, you will not be truly fed.

An entrepreneur like Brian Faherty, founder and creative director of Schoolhouse Electric & Supply Co., knows the power of cultivating a quiet space. Faherty founded his wildly successful company on the premise of returning to a handcrafted industrial lighting and home aesthetic. In a few short years, his company grew out of a small storefront into a 125,000-square-foot headquarters. He created a "digital-free zone" in his offices and named it the "Fire + Water room." Faherty found that balance between his digital and analog world was crucial to being a more effective leader and creative thinker. "I only have so much bandwidth myself, and if too much of it gets used up doing digital things, then I don't have any room left for the other areas that are more important to me." With a wood-burning stove set against a weathered brick wall and couches sporting wool blankets, the Fire + Water room is designed as a retreat for "the creative mind to work unencumbered by technology." Anyone who enters must leave digital devices behind, but they are welcome to add wood to the fire.[12]

Consider finding quiet space in your own way each day, with electronics set aside. Setting down distractions and nurturing a connection with your inner creative space is a loving act toward the creative potential within. If this inner place has been neglected, it may feel awkward at first to be in this stillness, requiring effort not to be pulled by outer distractions. But in the quiet is where you reconnect with your own creative impulses. Build in creative space and time in your life—even schedule it on your calendar—in order to reconnect with the inner muse and wellspring of your creativity. And once you find the inner stillness, stay in contact with it. In the words of Deepak Chopra, "Wherever you go in the midst of movement and activity, carry your stillness within you. Then the chaotic movement around you will never overshadow your access to the reservoir of creativity, the field of pure potentiality."[13]

Where is the quiet space in your home?
Where is the quiet moment in your day or week ahead?
How will you carry your stillness with you?

Too Many Inspirations versus Focused Fire

Though creativity requires inspiration, having too many interests can actually dilute creative energy so that nothing of substance is created or sustained. Realistically, a person can only effectively nurture two or three creative projects. Any more than that and there is not enough energy moving in a steady direction. And jumping from one creative idea to another without taking the time to develop a full creation means that creative potential is never fully realized.

Like a crop tended until harvest, what we cultivate is meant to nourish us, but it can only do so if we bring it to the point of full development. Make a choice about how you want to focus your creative energy, choosing two to three specific ways, and then build them into something lasting and real by giving them your focused attention over an extended period of time.

What is your creative focus for today?
What are your top three creative priorities for this year?

Overemphasis on Production versus
Refueling the Creative Well

The typical overemphasis on production limits creativity in multiple ways. A person who feels valuable when accomplishing tasks may have difficulty devoting time to a creative task that is not linked to visible production. Also, creativity tends to run in cycles of ebb and flow. As previously outlined, constant production usually leads to burnout and uninspired products rather than true creative inspiration; whereas making time for replenishment can ultimately fuel creativity in the long run.

Review your daily patterns: do you make lists that never end or forget to take vacations because you are too busy being productive? If so, shift your energy. Make sure that busy periods align with the seasons when you have more energy; add vacations and definitive rest periods in between. Downtime refills the creative well but also invites new insights and direction. The more you move in a cyclical manner, the more your natural creative flow will be both restorative and efficiently productive.

How will you refill your creative well today?
How might you replenish your creative well over the next month?

Dimming the Potential versus Revealing Your Radiance

Being creative and possessing your creative potential make you more radiant and visible to others. Unless you already feel comfortable in the light, you may avoid being creative in order to deflect the attention it can bring. Women often learn to place value outside of themselves for this reason. Men more readily step into the power of their potential but may overidentify with the provider role rather than making room for what they love. Either way, noticing how you stand in or avoid attention is critical for accessing your creative greatness. Again, areas of shame might be obscuring untapped potential. Changing core patterns and reclaiming creative potential require stepping outside of your comfort zone.

All people have a natural radiance that is more visible when they are using their creativity. Though we may want to become more visibly radiant, we typically learn to live in a particular range of comfort. We may have a natural tendency that is influenced by our early imprints and life experiences that form our way of being. We come to embody these expectations for ourselves, being visible in certain aspects and only within a particular range. To redefine that range, we first have to overcome our resistance to change. Then we must move beyond the range we inhabit, which, though it may feel normal and comfortable, can be less than our potential.

Using energy tools, ritual, and blessings can all be helpful in moving through the resistance you may encounter in expanding your range.

For example, when you take a creative risk or allow yourself to be more visible, you may feel unease or feelings of not being worthy of this much creative capacity. When this happens, do the "Attuning Your Energy–Body Interface" exercise (page 44) or the ritual below for "Sending Resistance to the Fire." Remember that you are changing your inner energy framework, and using energy-sensing meditations or rituals can assist your ability to embody the new potential in your creative field. It will be difficult to think your way there or talk yourself through it as this is not a mental process; rather, it is an energy shift and requires applied energy-medicine tools to change your core pattern.

As you work at the edges of your creative range and stretch into new modes or levels of radiance, you may also find that your loved ones or colleagues are uncomfortable with the changes because they will not recognize you at first. Like coming into the light from a dark room, it can be startling, uncomfortable, even irritating—for yourself and others—to change set patterns. But it ultimately means more access to your full creative-energy field and new capacity for brilliance.

> *What form is your radiance taking?*
> *How would you like to reveal more of your radiance?*
> *Where do you notice resistance to having an expanded creative range?*

Exercise: Sending Resistance to the Fire

This next exercise is designed for working with the resistance that often arises when you reclaim your creative range. You can do this on your own or with others. Find a quiet place, a pad of paper, and a pen to reflect.

1. Examine the resistance and the form in which it arises (for example, tension in the body, a sense of unworthiness, avoiding what needs to be done, or ignoring desires). As you reflect, locate the sensation that it relates to in your body and energy field.

2. Take a sheet of paper and write out all of your resistance in words. Examples: *I am not worthy. Who am I to take up this space? I don't really need this whole range. I'm afraid of stepping into this potential. Someone will think I'm selfish. This is stupid. I'm wasting my time. I don't have much to offer. I'm asking for too much.* Write for as long as necessary. Notice the contraction in your body and energy field that comes from facing this resistance, and then imagine freeing yourself from this diminished potential.

3. If you have a place for a contained fire, make one. Fold the paper multiple times and place it in the fire. Watch it burn. Let your resistance transmute in the fire. If you don't have a place for a fire, take the paper and tear it into many pieces, imagining that the element of fire breaks apart its hold. Take the pieces and bury them in the earth; release your resistance to the earth. Feel the release in your body and energy field.

4. As your resistance is transformed, notice the new freedom in your center. Make an imprint of the spaciousness in your body–energy sensations as ground fertile for planting your dream seeds.

5. Write down two to five intentions, such as *May I expand beyond my resistance to discover new capacity. May I revel in my radiance. May I receive the blessing of my own creative field. May I be a strong and powerful creative. May I reclaim my creative range.* From the ashes, allow your phoenix to rise and inspire new forms.

How Untapped Creativity Relates to Realizing Dreams

Wherever you have unrealized dreams, there are an untapped flow of creative currency and unexplored aspects of your creative-energy field. As you restore the flow of creative currency in your body and daily life and work with creative blocks to discover new creative range, prepare for your dreams to come into focus and then into being.

Energy Session: Embodying Her Natural Brilliance

When Clarissa came to my practice, she felt creatively blocked and wanted an energy session to understand why she was unable to move forward with her professional and personal dreams. I invited her to bring her focus to the pelvic bowl, where many people carry root patterns that inform their creativity. Unless these patterns are directly examined, they often remain unconscious, meaning that they are still governing access to energy without our clear awareness of them.

Clarissa brought her focus to the pelvic bowl, where we imprint our earliest sense of safety, security, and belonging (mainly from our tribe or family). Clarissa's focus would come down for a brief second and then jump back up toward her head. I told her that in order to bring her awareness to the bowl and maintain focus there, she would have to make the choice to be fully present in the moment and in her body. People who had a difficult early childhood may not want to be where they are, and will try to escape by shifting their awareness (and energy) away from the body (physical realm) and family-of-origin reality. When I brought to Clarissa's consciousness that she could make the choice to be here *now*, tears filled her eyes.

I asked Clarissa if her childhood had been challenging, and she said that there had been fighting and conflict from her earliest memories. She had learned to hide away—to be less visible in order to avoid the stress within her home. To Clarissa, home was equated with fear, anxiety, and stress; and this was reflected as a stress pattern in her root. Though she had long lived away from her family as an adult, early patterns informed the way she inhabited her body. I suggested that since her home and family stress was now gone and she had made new life patterns for herself, she could let the energy of her center come into this present time where there was peace, and adopt a new core pattern to reflect this. Until Clarissa was fully living from her center, it would be difficult for her to access the creative energy it contained to realize her dreams. When people are unable to manifest something (for example, they are not able to find the partner they desire, the job they want, or success in some manner or another), I find that they have given up their creative ground; they are not fully inhabiting their creative-energy field because of past wounds or energy imprints. Clarissa's creative block was the imprinted stress of her childhood, which was still limiting her ability to be in her own center, let alone use its creative energy.

I invited Clarissa to clarify her energy field by breathing from her core and down into the earth anything that no longer served her, sweeping the energy from her creative core in her mind's eye (using the following exercise). As she focused on her core, she remarked, "The energy is constricted and barren here. It looks nothing like the life I actually have." Indeed, the energy she released felt cold and contracted, like a harsh wind.

Tuning in to a person's core-energy field, I find that most people have a field that reflects (unconsciously) the patterns of energy in the home where they first imprinted what it means to be in a body. However, by becoming aware of and then intentionally releasing the old energy imprints—using energy-medicine tools such as energy-sensing meditations or rituals—these early imprints that constrict the creative field can be changed into patterns of creative flow and resonance. In this way, the creative field reforms to better reflect and support the creative potential of a person's present life.

After clarifying her energy field, I invited Clarissa to feel and sense her present reality from her center and notice how much had changed. Frequently, we live in the present yet embody the energy patterns from our past. One way to orient the body to present time is to become aware of all the subtle layers of sensation in the present moment. Sensing in this way, with focused awareness, can assist the body and energy field in attuning with the reality of now. This is why mindfulness exercises—practices that help us notice the sensations and awareness of the moment—are powerful. They are energy-medicine tools that shift and align energy patterns in beneficial ways.

As Clarissa began to feel the reality of her present life by sensing it with her core body, she came to a place of ease in her center. After several minutes of breathing into the new pattern, the constriction in her center released into a pulsing radiance like that found in a pristine place in nature. Clarissa said, "It's like a gem with facets shining in every direction. No wonder I wasn't feeling creative with that old pattern in my center. This is going to change everything." With this new presence and awareness in her core, I invited her to set an intention for her creative life in this powerful center point.

Clarissa stated her intention: to embody the ease of her natural brilliance. And by releasing this imprinted pattern of stress, she would also have more resilience in the face of stress. Instead of operating from her past stressed energy field, Clarissa could let the radiance within shape her daily experiences. She was well on her way to moving beyond these blocks that had diminished her creativity to inhabit a new way of being in her body, creative core, and life.

Exercise: Clarifying the Creative Field

Find a quiet place to reflect, ideally outside or near a window.

1. Bring awareness to your own center. Notice what is held here. See if your energy feels clear, like a tended place, or less clear. Without intentional tending, the center can accumulate energy much like a room gathers dust. Clarifying the creative field can enhance core flow.
2. After assessing your center, begin to clear this space. First imagine a connection from the center of yourself down into the earth, and re-establish a link to the wild. This is a way of grounding your energy field and giving the energy a place to go.
3. Now imagine walking around your energy field in a circle. Clarify your energy by brushing anything in need of clearing down toward the earth. Simply say to yourself, *I release the energy of anything I no*

longer need. You might envision yourself sweeping with a broom, or washing with water, clarifying the energy around your field and then embodying this new clarity.

4. When your energy field feels clear, relax into this new space. Like a tidied-up closet or a clean room, the energy space will feel lighter and more open. Notice the sensations from your center and connect with the beauty around you, of which you, too, are a part.

5. Now envision what qualities or images you want to hold in this newly clarified place: ease, peace, radiance, strength, abundance, a bountiful garden, more time in nature, health, vitality, relaxation, permission to dream or express your full potential—whatever you desire to hold in the potency of your creative center. Give thanks for your own bright energy field.

Creative Thinking and Abundance

In our culture, it's all too common to disassociate creativity and money. Either you make money and forgo your dreams or you live your dreams while struggling financially. Yet there is an essential correlation between creative thinking and abundance, as well as techniques for using this relationship strategically. For example, I had the opportunity to work with a developer on a house project. He was surprised that my husband and I would spend extra money to replace old electrical wiring (even though we couldn't see it) and upgrade our kitchen counters to a natural soapstone material; for him, cost was the primary measure of value. For us, health and beauty in the home were a higher priority than cost (within reason). We knew that spending a little more up front to have a healthy and aesthetically pleasing home would increase our overall energy abundance, and pay daily dividends well into the future.

Any challenge can become an asset when approached in a creative manner. In our household, for example, my sons are encouraged to find creative solutions when they encounter a challenge or want something that is not easily attainable. As an entrepreneur myself, I have developed my practice and books on the basis of creative thinking, and have provided many aspects of abundance for my family—even in the face of what first appear to be limitations. Limitations may inspire a new business model or better ways to integrate home and work life, particularly when you follow personal inspiration rather than well-intended counsel, formulas, or expectations from others.

A female naturopathy student told me that her class had received business advice and training from a prominent local naturopath who recommended that women who planned to have children delay child-bearing for at least five years and invest their energy and resources into building a large private practice. The problem with such a rigid for-mula is that if a woman develops an expensive practice, she will be beholden to all of those expenses even after she has a child. Prior to having children, few people realize how much hands-on time is called for in parenting and that they will likely value the freedom to make active choices about their work schedule without any added burden of debt.

If I had placed either dream on hold—having my own health-care practice or being a present mother to my children—these dreams might not be realized today. Instead, I followed the creative flow in my center and created what I desired both in terms of work and personal life as parts of a creative whole. However, to have business success, I had to shift my own limited thinking. Initially, I did not really think I could earn substantial income concurrently with mothering and was surprised when my private practice ultimately surpassed my salaried income (with fewer hours but a higher rate per hour). Building my business and parenting practice from the center of my life has been a continual exercise in creative thinking and expansion beyond perceived limitations.

One key to my own private practice success was maximizing value while minimizing overhead. I first rented a small office, the least expen-sive one in my office building, and often sublet it to further decrease expenses while I incrementally built the business. As my children grew and my schedule became more flexible, I concurrently expanded my business expenses and capacity for growth; I began teaching as part of my work. The teaching led to writing, which led to additional teaching, adding to our income and the abundant creative current that now ran through our home. At some point, I recognized that I actually could have the schedule I desired and mother my children every day. I could work in tandem with my husband so he could stay with his passion in the environmental field (without having to go back to a corporate job) while still receiving the income to sustain our family—and be able to do so by dwelling near the channel of these creative currents.

Creative thinking can generate new and expanded business concepts that not only solve problems but enhance business operations. Initially, I only received payments from clients by check—until accepting credit cards became easy, thanks to the creativity of Jack Dorsey. Dorsey, the creative mind behind the microblogging tool Twitter, invented Square to help an artist friend who was missing out on sales because he lacked options for receiving credit-card payments. An ingenious product that allows anyone to receive a credit-card payment through a smartphone, Square has allowed me to accept credit cards at my office and has revolutionized payment and sales for many other small-scale entrepreneurs, such as food carts, artisans, music teachers, and yoga teachers.

Dorsey has an affinity for simplicity and efficiency, as illustrated by his concept of brief "tweets" as instant communication. Twitter was designed to converse in real time as something was occurring, and it has become a force of its own in breaking news and in the political arena—a valuable marketing tool. And Twitter evolved as people used it and discovered new potential.

Dorsey's products are reminiscent of the first iPods in their simplicity and untapped potential for transforming and disrupting (in a good way) how things are done in business and daily life. Both Square and iPods are examples of how business success follows naturally when the products or services break through a limitation in the overall creative range.

Energy Session: Finding a New Money-Making Strategy

Abbie came for a session to address her financial picture. A few years earlier, she had left a corporate job in order to fulfill her dream of teaching yoga, but she was having difficulty sustaining her livelihood. Living one's dreams often requires using creative energy to generate a whole new life structure. First I asked where her primary stress was. Abbie answered that it was paying her mortgage on a three-bedroom home. The house was more space than she needed, but she loved her neighborhood. Then I asked where her place of ease was. She named several things: having the freedom in her schedule outside of a for-ty-hour workweek, teaching yoga, and working in her yard.

I invited Abbie to bring awareness to her own center and expand her creative-energy field to envision a new money-making strategy. We imagined her house and asked how to make it more financially viable. Abbie had been contemplating the renovation of a large garage on her property into something called an "Accessory Dwelling Unit," a planning term for another structure on a property. Because she felt overwhelmed by financing the project, she hadn't made any specific plans; but her inner guidance brought her immediately to this pos-sibility. I asked how she might find out more, and she said there was a class she could take to learn about creative financing for these types of buildings. The idea was to renovate a smaller space to live in using a small loan, then to rent out the larger property to cover the primary mortgage. This would take some effort and planning but could address Abbie's main area of stress by paying her mortgage.

In my clients, I've seen how creative energy can solve financial challenges. For example, when someone is using only linear-based thinking to assess a situation, they perceive limited choices. In contrast, the creative field brings a plethora of options and a holistic perspective. It invites transformation of early imprints of scarcity that would otherwise limit imagination or access to what is possible. This inner knowledge can also help a person craft the form for an idea. Dreams are ethereal by nature, but for dreams to become real, they also need a solid form. Sometimes dreams are out of touch with reality, like that of a client who wanted to "write a bestseller" even though she had no active writing practice. Bringing the essence of a dream into earth-based reality is a creative art.

Abbie's inner creative flow was directing her to a solution that was already within her reach if she would take the next steps. I invited her to ask herself what was holding her back. She reflected and then answered, "It's a sense of being overwhelmed in doing something new and unknown. But if I take a class and follow the guidance from others who've been through the process, I can see that it's doable and potentially even exciting. I could still enjoy my neighborhood, my garden, my freedom, and my yoga without the financial burden." She noted that as rents increased in certain neighborhoods, some people even made a monthly income this way. Abbie had taken a step in the direction of her dreams by teaching yoga; now she could use the inspiration of her creative field to build a money plan for sustaining herself and her dreams.

Parenting and Creative/Entrepreneurial Thinking

Creative and entrepreneurial thinking can be started and developed in childhood. I have learned to appreciate the importance of creative thinking in making a life and work that I love, and I know it can be taught. My husband, Dan, and I regularly invite our sons to think creatively. For Dan, this means showing them how to take initiative and solve problems as well as work in the context of community. For my part, I focus on the creative-energy field. I want my sons to be aware of their core creative flow and desires, as well as how to access the whole creative field. I encourage them to use both feminine and masculine fields by using the "being" and "doing" aspects of themselves. I praise their feminine creative expression and celebrate the robust masculine that arises in its presence. I educate them about maintaining feminine–masculine balance with cyclical versus linear modes of being. I also model this in my life for my sons to witness. For example, after a busy four-day workshop where my outer, masculine, right energy field has been working in overdrive to produce and teach a class, I subsequently prioritize the importance of rest. Even though I have emails and other work to catch up on, I drop my business agenda in favor of ritual, connecting with a friend, having downtime with family, or engaging in other feminine, left-energy-field activities to restore my overall balance.

Though my sons do not have the energy of an actual womb that females do, I show them how to set intentions for themselves and place them into earth, either with an energy meditation in their mind's eye or an actual ritual of writing their intentions and placing them into the ground. I teach them to listen for the next creative direction from within their own center by knowing how to sense the creative flow.

Parents have the first impact on the nurturing or stifling of creative impulses in children. Mary Mazzio produced *Lemonade Stories*, an unusual documentary that explains the extraordinary connection between entrepreneurs such as Richard Branson and their mothers. Highlighting a link between parenting and creativity in children, she points out that parents have a direct impact on "sparking creativity and entrepreneurial spirit in their children." As she says, "My own opinion . . . is that entrepreneurs can be made—and that parents play a central role in making them."[14]

She recognized that in her parenting she had had a tendency to compensate for any of her children's challenges, attempting to ease their way, until her interview with Eve Branson for the documentary. Eve refused to accept Richard's "disabling" shyness and forced him to interact with others in the world. Rather than explaining away his discomfort and inadvertently reinforcing it, she dropped him off three miles from home one day (at age seven) and told him to talk to other people to find his way home. While this technique would not work in this age of parenting, Mazzio recognized that there was an important lesson in Branson's long walk that influenced her own parenting from that point on.

Mazzio shifted her perspective and began to challenge her children in new ways so they might grow into potential as yet unrealized. Mazzio's discovery caused me to pause as well: *Where was I allowing my children to be less than whole simply because something was hard for them?* Providing nourishment for our children does not mean avoiding the challenges that can assist their development. There is an essential truth here: parents can engage their children in a way that fosters resilience and creativity in order to expand that capacity.

Parents are uniquely placed to provide the initial and then routine dose of encouragement for creative thinking. Parents can also provide that all-powerful faith in their child's creative abilities. Who has not been impacted by what a parent thinks of his or her capacity to succeed (or fail) at something? Likewise, the more visibly parents use creativity in their lives, the more they will inspire and model the benefits and possibilities of engaging creativity as a way of life.

Owning the Wild Creative

Regardless of the parenting we receive, we must eventually own the potential we contain to give our creative selves both the encouragement and the range to take full form. We can provision ourselves with whatever we may not have previously been given in order to step into this full creative field, remembering that the energy meant to move through us has its own unique expression.

Creative energy can seem to require sanction; and though we may have the notion that we require this validation from the outer world (parents, employers, friends, media, and others), we must give permission to be creative to ourselves first and foremost. We must believe and know in our deepest sense of self, that what arises through us is beautiful and essential—truly worthy of expression. We can take note of where others have failed to notice or encourage this potential in us; but ultimately, it is in recognizing our own potential that we gain access to this wildly creative current within.

Reshape Your Creative Imprints

Vision and potential gestate in the feminine realm, and tangible form is made by engaging the masculine. Having one without the other leads to creative obstruction. On the other hand, creative manifestation only arises from a personal connection to both realms and by tapping into the whole creative-energy field. A person may try to resolve creative frustration by changing the external circumstances of their life—pursuing a new job, a new partner, a new exercise routine. But time and again, the solution to feeling creative lies within. *Do I know what brings my creativity to life and how I might access that potential?* This is the question that will change the way you feel and ultimately the way you live.

One day when we were in our twenties, my best friend, Sara, and I were visiting together and decided to have a tarot reading with an intuitive. For Sara's reading, she asked several questions about her career path. Listening to her questions, I was puzzled by her exclusive focus on the professional realm, but my professional identity was less developed at the time. When it was my turn for a reading, I asked about my future children and life as a mother. Our male reader, who was a great model of using the feminine creative in his readings, pulled card after card about fertility and mothering. I would later discover that I was already pregnant with my first child. Mothering was on my horizon but remained the furthest thing from Sara's mind. When I look back at that moment from our current perspective, both of us mothers and professionals now, I see that we were each seeking guidance about our creative energy in our own way.

Since we learn about creativity and creative potential from our earliest formation in our mother's womb, and then during our time being mothered by her, our creative identity is rooted in these experiences. Though the creative center of the female body is a powerful generator of life, women are hardly living with a connection to this place. That means mothers aren't always aware of the imprints they are giving to their children that might counter their children's natural creative impulses. If lacking a connection to her core creative flow, a woman mothers from this imbalanced pattern; and her children imprint the imbalance. What she values creatively is also imprinted. In Sara's case, her mother was a natural homemaker but desired a life beyond the home. She longed for a professional identity provided by the outer (more masculine) world. Since she mothered with this longing, she encouraged her daughter to seek creative validation in the working world. Hence, her daughter initially found her creative bounty in a professional life, not knowing that she might also find it as a mother.

Meanwhile, my mother had initially identified her joy with having children. In contrast to the feminist orientation of the time and of women seeking life outside the home, my mother focused her attention on the home and a desire to have children. Though I would later see her pursue other creative pursuits in order to feel more personally fulfilled, my early encoding regarding creative purpose was deeply woven with the home. So I sought my answers regarding my creative life in becoming a mother and being in the home (though I had no idea how to bridge mothering and making an income, which would later prove to be necessary).

Though many gender roles are changing, men have routinely been encouraged to shape their lives around making a profession and earning an income instead of listening to the creative muse within. For both genders, how we were mothered and how our mothers approached mothering affect our core sense of self and the value we imprinted regarding our creative essence. And this lays down the core imprint for the way we engage creativity in our lives.

However, creative potential does not have to be limited to one place, such as in the home or the outer world, or in relationship to gender roles; rather, it can always be accessed in our own center. Though we may have learned otherwise, creative potential does not have to be defined by what we are doing—whether we have a career or children, or whether we are in the home or at work. Instead, this energy current that moves through us is our birthright. It is the energy pulse with which we must be in touch in order to feel creatively alive. And again, the truth is that for creative purpose to be actualized, we need a connection from our center to both the feminine inner world (to receive the energy) and the masculine outer world (to give it form); we must strike a balance between the two to engage our whole creative self.

Exercise: Attuning to Both the Feminine and Masculine Creative Realms

Creativity comprises both a feminine internal aspect and a masculine external aspect. To examine your relationship with these parts of the creative whole, find a pen, a pad of paper, and a quiet place where you can reflect.

1. Make a list of all the feminine visioning/dreaming/fluid aspects of your creativity that come to mind. How do you receive and nourish inspiration?
2. Make a list of the masculine aspects of your creativity that involve making or shaping a particular form or visible expression. How do you express your inspiration?
3. Do you access both the feminine and masculine realms equally or in the way you would like? Are there any areas of expression that feel

blocked for you? How might a feminine or masculine trait enable you to change this imprint or have more creative flow?

4. Take a moment to sense the left energy field on the left side of your body, where the feminine resides, and then the right energy field on the right side of your body, where the masculine aspects reside. After doing this, see if anything else comes to mind for tapping into these realms.

5. Choose two things from each list to focus on and expand your routine access to both the feminine and masculine creative realms. Give thanks for both your feminine and masculine natures.

Energy Session: Reviving Feminine Modes of Production

Emma came for an energy session to rejuvenate herself. She was an entrepreneur feeling overwhelmed by her business as a fitness instructor, finding herself less in touch with her own health as her business expanded. When we began the session, I invited Emma to notice that all of her focus and energy presence was on the right side of her body and pelvic bowl, with an absence of energy on the left side. She mentioned that her left side even felt numb.

I asked Emma about her primary stress, as she was demonstrating a pattern of imbalance, with the right side (the masculine field that engages when we have tasks to accomplish) hyperengaged in overdoing and the left side (the feminine field where we are meant to receive equal to what we give) lacking in much-needed replenishment. Emma answered that her stress arose from the feeling that everything was her responsibility. She had always prided herself on being resourceful and strong, but as she had more to do, she also felt more overwhelmed. She did not know how to prioritize her many work demands, and her own health was not a current priority. Even talking about her workload increased her tension; she continued to place the additional load on her right, "overly capable" side. As her responsibilities grew, she met them with her achiever self, leaving less and less room for accessing her left side and her personal needs. All of the output, with little input, was bound to increase her sense of feeling burdened and depleted.

I asked Emma to focus her breath and awareness on the left side of her body and imagine giving time to this part of herself. In doing so, she reported a sense of guilt in making time for what felt "unproductive." She knew all of the demands on her time, and even turning to look at the left side felt like a waste to her. When a framework of using one's energy is so entrenched, it takes concerted effort to make a lasting change. I asked Emma if she could recognize that taking care of herself was the essential task. She could hardly run a company promoting wellness when she herself was so far out of relationship with her health. I hoped that if Emma could see how integral she was to the whole picture, she might be more motivated to change the energy pattern of how she was operating.

On an intellectual level, Emma knew that her own self-care was just as important, because her business was centered around health. Yet she felt trapped in her pattern of ignoring herself to get things done. Emma pondered this and stayed with her uncomfortable sense of resistance to being still and reflective in the session, as she was more comfortable focusing on the mountain of tasks she had to accomplish. Suddenly, she remembered a time when she was seven years old. She was playing in the backyard by herself, making up a story and looking at the clouds. Her mother yelled out the window that she needed her help and to "stop being lazy." The code in her family was work focused. In fact, there was a whole lineage pattern in her parents and grandparents that emphasized and valued nonstop work. There was also frequent stress around money, and her parents responded to this stress by working harder. There were no memories Emma could call to mind of open-ended time together or even laughter. As long as you were working and contributing something you were "good," idle time was not to be encouraged or trusted.

As Emma spent more time connecting with this feminine aspect of herself, she was reminded of that dreamy essence of childhood imagination, and her entire energy field felt more at ease. Emma loved reading, gardening, lying in the sun—but she rarely let herself truly indulge in these pleasures. She did allow herself exercise but limited it to running because it was quicker, when she really desired to attend a Nia or yoga class. Even in the act of running, she realized that she hardly felt the sensations in her body because she was focused on thinking about her project list. Emma had gone into fitness as a way of being healthier in her own life, but now she made the connection that the pressure she felt to be successful in business was causing her to resort to the family pattern of overwork. But Emma did not need to compromise her health to achieve success; that was an ingrained but false family pattern. If she could change her exercise program back to a less practical and more pleasurable format—and even pay attention to her body while doing so, instead of thinking about her to-do list—she would not only nourish herself but energize her feminine space, which is vital for the creative aspects of any business.

In her work, Emma was embodying the code of her family and approaching her daily tasks in a linear manner, emphasizing a masculine mode of doing, with no room for dreams or the feminine. While it can be helpful to have a list to organize what needs to be accomplished, using a more natural rhythm to guide productivity allows for the feminine. In fact, having a robust feminine presence brings creative insights and energy to the masculine aspects of building a business. Even taking short breaks for pleasure in the midst of a busy day will increase feminine energy. Ideally, the feminine and masculine aspects are engaged equally, yet this rarely happens unless we consciously make it so. Having Emma focus her attention on her left energy field increased the warmth and sensation in this space so that it was more even with her right side. As we discussed the integration of masculine and feminine approaches to daily rhythms, Emma had a clearer understanding of how to use these aspects of herself in a balanced way, such as scheduling time for self-nourishment and care and letting go of less important details in order to focus on the whole.

I invited Emma to set these intentions for herself in her creative core—to embody this new perspective. She started to do this, but then her energy field contracted. I asked how it was going, and she gave voice to the stress she felt: "I don't even know how to set my intentions or do it in a way that will ensure they happen." Emma was again reflecting an unbalanced, masculine approach. Rather than setting the intentions in the energy field and trusting the guidance of energy and spirit that comes from this inner creative space, Emma felt she had to personally do something or nothing would happen. Even worrying about how these intentions would manifest interfered with the energy. She was engaging the masculine *doing* aspect of self rather than the feminine *being* aspect.

When people have both creative intentions and complete trust in the process, their energy field has an overall resonance to it. As soon as they start trying to think about how something will occur, they begin to micromanage the energy, and their field becomes contracted and distressed. Placing intentions with full surrender and faith does not mean there is no work involved; it just means that you set the intentions as if they were already complete in that moment. Later, by staying in each moment, you walk step-by-step to the place of completion. This leaves room for the broader potential of the divine as guide and cocreator in the process. I told Emma about an architect I had worked with who felt that the projects she was more in alignment with tended to come her way when she herself was in alignment—that feeling vibrant and centered personally was good for her business. These are feminine modes of production.

I invited Emma to again place intentions in her center, such as *I intend to trust the flow of feminine energy to guide my life, to expand my potential by connecting to my full creative essence, and to receive what*

I need using my whole field of inspiration. She then blessed these intentions with *I am radiant. I am blessed. May these intentions be received. May I receive guidance to bring these intentions into form.* As Emma did this, her energy field broadened into a new form. Now she could begin to employ the potential of her whole creative field as nourishment for herself and her growing business.

Reflect on Your Creative Lineage

Whatever you may have learned about creativity in your family—what it is, how it is expressed, who has it, how to be creative (or not) in the midst of making a life—it needs to be sorted out in order to identify helpful patterns and reshape others. Since mothers in the past few generations typically overidentified with one creative aspect, or even blocked the masculine or the feminine entirely, there is a reshaping of patterns to be done. Likewise, fathers have had limited access to their authentic creativity because of cultural or family expectations to earn an income and provide financial support. And any family operating from a place of stress or scarcity may have been creative out of need, or perhaps discouraged creative impulses altogether.

Think about how creativity was expressed or restricted in your family and how it was encouraged or shaped for you. Ponder whether creative dreams were nurtured or critiqued. Notice how you and others in your family access creativity.

One of my neighbors is a successful novelist. He told me that when he was in the writing flow, he felt himself in a white sphere of light. This image is reminiscent of the creative energy of the womb space. By engaging our creative patterns, we can draw upon strengths and reshape limitations so that the lines guiding our creative impulses reflect our earliest potential, and better assist whatever we are making.

What is your creative lineage? How was creativity expressed in your family?

Were there any unrealized creative dreams in your family? How did these impact your creative life?

How would you like to change your inheritance or increase your creative flow?

To access more of your creative potential, first examine where you might already be naturally using it. Look for the ease and flow in your life. Notice patterns of success and lines of creative energy that may reflect a creative lineage. My vivid and hands-on creative life is one that I have developed for myself—but it has roots in observing my parents using creativity to transform patterns of financial poverty for themselves.

Just as the challenges of lineage can arise when we seek our creative essence, so can the strengths. When a musician in India announces that he is a fourth-generation tabla player, he is speaking to the power of lineage for developing creative potential. In the same manner, though no one was a healer in my immediate family, I have often felt that a powerful healing thread runs through my ancestral line. When I first began to place my hands on people, there was a sense of ancient knowing contained in my hands about where to work in order to bring healing. Each of us carries these potentials that we already know or have yet to discover.

Where do you utilize creative thinking or potential in your life?

What type of creative potential do you notice in your family?

Is there a creative thread you desire to explore or build upon?

Dealing with the Critical Voice

In exploring the creative range, it is normal to encounter a critical inner voice that may reflect family or cultural messages about being creative. In taking risks in order to make the life of your dreams, be prepared to meet the inner critic—but don't give it authority. To live creatively, pay more attention to creative impulses and less to the inner critic, especially when you are in the process of trying something new or are in the early stages when a creative process is vulnerable. When my husband and I were first dating, we had a long-distance relationship. We almost did not make it through that early courtship because I had no idea of the depth of his feelings for me. A year later, I moved to San Francisco to live with him. I opened his dresser drawer one day to find a stack of letters he had never sent to me because he was too critical of what he had written to share them. As a result, his mailed letters had been sparse in number and expression. It became our metaphor of creative expression: *Do not to keep your love letters hidden in a drawer lest you lose your love.*

Letting the critic be too strong can greatly reduce creativity and squelch our dreams. Give less credence to the critic within, and you give more room to creative expression. Almost anyone who makes something worthwhile has made the choice to place less stock in the critical voice and more in the creative one. Regardless of what you have learned from family or from a production-oriented culture, release the hold of criticism that would dampen creative courage and exploration. A relic of fear or shame, the critic is an unnecessary attempt to avoid the potential shame of being imperfect. One key is to focus more on the flow of creative energy instead of on the outcome or creation itself—to have more freedom simply to create and generate creative currency.

Additionally, reshaping your creative framework often requires new patterns of self-talk that give permission and encouragement to fully express yourself. The ultimate form of creative expression is to be who you truly are.

Make New Patterns

My family came from poverty, but both of my parents worked their way out of it by being creative. My mother was artistic and started a dance studio that served as both a creative outlet for her and a way of earning extra income for our family. My father was the first person in his family to attend college; and he even went on to receive a doctorate degree in finance, becoming a professor in that field. Having grown up in financial scarcity, he pursued his graduate degree in a field focusing on wealth creation. Later on, he was creative with property and found value in land where others missed it. He created wealth not only as a professor and an investor but also in property development. My parents made new money patterns for themselves over time, yet I still had a sense of scarcity from our early years of struggle, doubting my own ability to make money. Deep within my psyche, I had learned that money was scarce and difficult to come by.

The best antidote for changing scarcity imprints is by engaging them with creativity. As a new mother myself, I initially felt that I had limited options that consisted of either (a) working for a physical therapy practice that would set my hours and provide monetary security but offer little control over the time I spent with my child; or (b) staying home with my young child and being strapped financially. It seemed I could choose between security and limitation or freedom and risk. I was looking through a conventional lens that had only two options.

However, I could have approached this issue in a multitude of ways had I been thinking creatively. Eventually, an organic path toward starting my own practice opened my eyes to a holistic and creative perspective. As mentioned previously, when I started my health practice, I kept things simple by choosing a small office with low overhead. Rather than advertise, I received referrals by word of mouth to save even more money. With few expenses, it was easier than I had thought to work a financially rewarding part-time schedule while tending to the needs of my young children. I worked one weekday and one Saturday so my husband and I could trade off covering childcare; this worked well for our family and prevented the expense of day care. By being creative, I had the freedom to earn an income doing something I enjoyed and still be with my children much of the time.

Given our culture's messages about money, many of us have limited thinking patterns regarding how to earn an income or even to assess value. Yet when we feel connected to our inner creative, we naturally access the feminine realm that generates our creative currency. This is the space where dreams are free to roam, time and money concerns and other limitations fade, and you feel intimately intertwined with the energy of life. Here, the linear world of limited possibilities drops away and you can "lose yourself" in this flow. Every person should know how to embrace this part of themselves—the place where they feel alive and purposeful without making something or needing to achieve a particular outcome. If you already know how to connect with this place for yourself, make whatever brings you there a priority in your life: gardening, cooking, meditating, walking, writing, dancing, and so on. Making routine contact with your flow of creative currency is essential for broadening your creative bandwidth and generating new patterns of being. This is the place of raw ideas and inspiration, where creative insights enter. Creativity and creative insights solve many problems and offer many solutions in our lives, from money scarcity to work issues to family challenges to realizing our dreams and beyond. I invite you to engage your creative flow in response to any limitation you encounter and simply make a new pattern.

> *What creative pursuits connect you to your creative currency and your energy of life?*
> *What limiting concepts do you hold about having a career, making an income, or other seemingly fixed aspects of your life?*
> *How might you engage creativity to make a new pattern instead?*

The Spirit Door and the Birth Field

Each of us came into being through the womb. It is the original spirit door, where spirit becomes the unique form of you. Again, some of the earliest creative imprints for both genders reside in our connection to the mother's womb, not only during gestation in our mother's body but also in the birth process (including adoption). While we are forming our bodies and making our passage into life, we often imprint the creative framework and other family patterns that form our creative capacity, depending on how we were birthed or parented. Likewise, when someone is accessing the creative field by using their creative energy, it very much resembles the energy pattern of a beautifully aligned or resonant pelvic bowl—this first creative field we inhabited.

A powerful means of making a new core pattern and resolving any limitations is to work with realigning the birth field: the potent energy field around us at birth that informs our entry. I include energy-sensing meditations for mothers to realign the birth field for their children in my second book, *Mothering from Your Center*. I have witnessed profound shifts in women's bodies for healing difficult births, birth loss, and bonding disruptions when they use these birth-field energy tools. There are several real stories about women's experiences with this type of healing in my mothering book, where we interfaced with the energy imprint in order to realign birth fields that did not achieve their fullness. A natural and undisturbed birth creates a resonant birth field; but when there is intervention, trauma, or stress, this energy process can be interrupted. In my work with women, I've found that the energy imprint can be changed and the birth field restored even years after the birth event.

One of the stories I write about involves healing birth through three generations. It begins with a woman whose grown daughter was close to conceiving her first grandchild. There had been an intervention that resulted in a cesarean in the daughter's birth, so her mother and I did a birth-energy realignment to change the imprint. The story relays the sequence of events, from doing the birth-field realignment meditation to the daughter's conception of her son later that same day; and the resulting healing birth event nine months later that passed from mother to daughter to grandson. The energy field of the birth door has potent medicine.

Regardless of the conception, pregnancy, birth, or parenting you had, you can work on the realignment of the birth field for yourself as an adult, reclaiming your full and rightful creative capacity. To do this, I recommend you find a place to sit in nature and use the energy-meditation exercise that follows.

Exercise: Realigning Your Birth Field

Find a place that comfortably holds your body and sit down. Call to mind "The Body's Creative-Energy Field" diagram (page 37). Think about how your mother's physical body and womb dilated for your entry when you were born. The energy center also dilates and expands toward the greater realm of spirit to receive your soul essence. Imagine holding the potential of that birth field for yourself, the bright crystal of your radiant creative potential. Now close your eyes to visualize.

1. Go outside, or imagine yourself sitting on the ground or leaning against a tall tree, surrounded by the energy of the earth. Let the earth energy around you serve as the Great Mother, the maternal essence that holds our full capacity regardless of the birth or mothering we received. Feel the sensation of the ground beneath you or the sky above—the earth energy containing your energy field. From your vantage point in the present moment, being held by the energy of the Great Mother, reflect on your soul essence and its first entry into a baby body.

2. Now let the energy around you expand into the support of the greater field, as if inhaling a big breath. Imagine that the wild is holding and aligning your energy so that the birth door—the energy opening in the creative field—can open for your fullest expression of self. Sense into or see the beauty of this aligned field around you. Let your birth field find its true form. Allow the air, ground, and light to increase the alignment between you and the greater field. Let the energy of your center embody this bright potential.

3. When the birth field (or imprinted energy field around you) feels aligned—like a feeling of calm or heightened clarity—sense into the flow of the birth energy that brought you into being like a stream of water. Sense it moving through this expanded field, touching the radiance it contains, and let it meet you here in present time. Allow this flow to infuse your cells and your body–energy interface with the potency of spirit energy that is your birthright. Let it activate your sacred potential in this moment. For those aspects within you that weren't mothered in the ways your spirit needed and that carry the inner child still longing to be met, may the Great Mother hold you today and every day so your radiance can bloom.

4. Open your eyes and sense the birth field flowing once more. Know that you carry this beauty of spirit enfolded within your body; remember the medicine and creative abundance it holds especially for you. Call it into your day as a divine embrace, and let it infuse all that you are making.

Claim Greater Potential

Every person has places of creative expansion and aspects of creative limitation. In addition to working with the places of natural creativity, we can step further into areas that are fraught with challenge in order to claim more potential. For example, I am creatively challenged by cooking. Over the years, I have worked with this in different ways. Most successfully, I have learned from several women friends how to cook a few key dishes. By learning to cook a traditional lasagna from a friend who long ago mastered this art, I feel more expansive myself. And though I still do not feel the creative freedom I would like in the kitchen, being willing to work at my creative edge has ultimately enabled me to claim more creative potential overall by increasing my comfort with creative risks and with new forms of expression.

While the tendency is to avoid your limitations, try seeking creative solutions in response to limitations in order to claim more potential.

Rather than offering excuses for not engaging creativity—such as being too busy with parenting, a demanding job, or the details of life—make creativity a priority, finding what works best at each phase in your life.

Writing is an important part of my creative expression, but after my third child was born, I could scarcely dress myself each day, let alone write in a consistent manner. I decided to write one line of reflection on motherhood each day. For the next year, at the end of every evening, my writing consisted of one line. (One of these held the title for a future book: *December 4th: Mothering from my center, I become more of who I truly am and create what it is that my heart desires.*)

I found this miniature writing task both doable and inspiring, and I savored the quiet ritual at the close of my day. The brief format meant that I had to distill my thoughts into a stream of words like poetry (and this was before the abbreviated inspiration of Twitter). I cherish this small book, this record of one line of thought for each day—even though many lines detail a tangible exhaustion—because I stayed true to my creative practice in the midst of our first year with three children.

Once you begin to access your creative essence in the more challenging places, the overall creative flow will build upon itself.

Where do you feel creatively blocked or limited in creative expression? How might you engage this block or limitation in order to receive more potential?

Energy Session: Finding a New Creative Direction

Sandy came for an energy session to receive inner wisdom in regard to finding a new direction in her life. For more than a decade, she had been a mental health counselor for a government agency. She felt increasingly burned out from her clients' high needs and the scarce resources available to address them. When we tuned in to her center, the energy felt weighted, as if she were carrying a burden. Though

Sandy wanted to move into private practice, she mentioned that she was staying in her present job for the security it offered. I asked her to imagine a day at her job. The sense of heaviness increased in her center. Reflecting upon this increase in energy density, I suggested to Sandy that the structure of support and security that her current employment provided was primarily a mental one. In reality, her body only felt the burden of spending her days at this particular job.

I encouraged Sandy to imagine the job of her dreams by creating a vision of the type of office she might like to have, the clients she might work with, and even her ideal schedule. Rather than limiting herself in any way, I asked her to simply imagine as fully as possible her dream work situation. Dreaming a new form for herself was the first step in actually creating it. As she created this image in her mind's eye, her body energy became light and responsive. The weighted feeling dissipated and she noticed a sense of renewed energy in her center. She remarked, "This is the best I've felt. I've wanted to start my own counseling practice, but I have no business skills, and it seems over-whelming to begin. But I can feel the difference when I allow myself to see the full vision of it—like I can find my way to what I imagine."

While starting her own counseling practice would mean leaving a known work structure, trading it for the unknown of building a business and the steps that would entail, the energy shift in Sandy's center was clear validation of a potentially lighter and more satisfying path. At first, there would be the work of establishing an office and a clientele, as well as addressing the business and legal issues of her practice; but the relief in her body from being in a new and healthier environment with better-resourced clients would more than make up for the workload. Eventually, once her practice was established, her core energy would be free to expand her practice in the direction of her desires.

Sandy acknowledged the relief she was already experiencing and knew it was a signal from her inner wisdom. She had been wanting to make a work change for some time but kept putting it off. Her new inner awareness motivated her to follow through on her plans to leave her job and begin a private practice. Though it was intense work, by the time Sandy returned to my office a year later, she was a new person. She was happily self-employed in her private practice and her energy reflected the health of that change. The weight in her center was gone, and the creative flow was vibrant and strong. She had envisioned a work structure that now sustained her—one that provided both the income and the energy currency for living.

Though you may hesitate to leave the comfort of what is known in some particular aspect of your life—whether in work, relationships, or your own way of engaging the world—when your energy is burdened by these outdated structures, it is time for a transition. Following the creative impulse, you can reshape or make new structures to support your robust creative health for the long term.

Use the Vast Potential of the Heart

Love what you do and do what you love. This folk wisdom recognizes that the heart has potency and power to transcend the biggest obstacles and limiting imprints—if only we are able to engage life from the heart rather than the head. Reflect on the following questions to encourage the creative flow in the heart:

- What do you absolutely love in your life right now?
- What do you love that you wish you had more access to?
- How would your life be different if you were living from the creative flow of the heart?

Keep Your Focus in the Now

As the last rays of sunset filtered through the grapevines one autumn day, I paused to refill my energy by savoring the golden light. When I drop into a moment of pure presence, it is as if my sons sense this and seek me out. I had just closed my eyes and turned my face toward the sun when my oldest son poked his head out the back door.

"Hey, Mom, want to have a popsicle with me?"

"No thanks on the popsicle, but I will enjoy your company if you want to sit with me."

"Would you rather have an ice cream bar?" he asked.

"Sure, an ice cream bar sounds good. Let's share one."

He disappeared, but a moment later, popped his head back out. "Are you sure you don't want a popsicle?"

I opened my eyes and looked at him. My inner peace was dissipating with these interruptions, but I sensed a teaching moment. I paused from my own point of stillness to see him.

"Honey, what do you really want?" I asked.

He began an elaborate dialogue about how many popsicles and ice cream bars there were, and how they might be divided if his brothers were to return home from their walk and have a treat too. In a less-centered moment, I might have been pulled off track by the chattering, but instead, I stopped him:

"Honey, what do you really want *right now, in this moment*?"

"A popsicle," he answered without hesitation.

"There you go. Keep your focus in the now—decide what you want right now and go from that place."

He was talking about a popsicle, but this simple formula of focusing in the now is helpful for making decisions in life, avoiding distractions, and staying clear about true desires. Several hours later, when one of his brothers was trying to decide about the dessert options and how they might be divided up over the next day or two, I heard my oldest say, "Keep your focus in the now."

Staying focused on the present sounds simple, but there are reasons it is challenging to keep your attention in this central place. It may require a shift in how you embody your energy field, as the next story illustrates.

Energy Session: Tending the Fire Within

Catherine came for an energy session as she was preparing to retire from her corporate career. Rather than looking forward to it, she found the thought of more free time disconcerting. Catherine recognized her attachment to the busyness of her life; with a self-described tendency to overextend herself at work, she was also the nurturer and problem solver for her family of origin and her grown children. Likewise, she fulfilled a caregiving role in her partnership and often with friends, routinely valuing what she could give more than receive. She took pride in not needing much for herself. Even if she did something she enjoyed, like gardening, she took on a large project and worked until she reached exhaustion. And she was feeling exhausted more frequently. As she prepared to make a life change, her patterns of overdoing were clearly taking a toll; but her identity and sense of personal value were so interconnected with them that she did not know how to change.

I brought the session's focus to Catherine's center, which was difficult to locate because she resided mostly outside of it. Her entire energy framework was built on making projects happen and taking care of others—until she was entirely out of touch with her own needs. Her self-denial was a longtime pattern of dysfunction, but it was now more clearly visible as she stepped out of her professional role and came back to herself.

As Catherine worked to maintain her focus on the center, she was surprised to find how much effort it took. I explained to her that each family member or work project or friend who called her away from her center was like an energy line she followed away from herself. She had so many of these that she had no boundaries for staying within herself, and the energy in her core was dispersed. I suggested she try imagining that she was making one bright fire in her center and keeping all of her attention there. Then I asked her to let the fire expand and, rather than taking care of multiple external factors, to invite others to sit by the warmth of her core.

Catherine recognized that it was long past time to tend this inner fire. Sitting by the fire within herself, she felt fear arise that if she was not busy, resources would become scarce. On a deeper level, the busyness kept her from dealing with the root fear of scarcity. Yet she wanted to shift the pattern of overdoing and savor the abundance of her life. When she recognized this truth, the energy filled her center with warmth. Catherine was a creative generator. By focusing the majority of her attention on being with herself first and charting her new creative journey, she would build a solid framework for the next phase of her life. The best gift we have for ourselves is to give light to our brightest fire; and the best gift we can give to others is to share the warmth it creates, not by dispersing it but by carefully tending the fire within.

Earth and Spirit Medicine

If you find it difficult to return to your center and maintain your presence there, I recommend spending time in the natural world. It is true that we are facing a "nature deficit disorder," the term Richard Louv uses in his book *Last Child in the Woods*, which explores the growing trend of children (and adults) spending less time outdoors and the problems that entails. This lack of time in nature and the overbusyness of our lives affect our very well-being.

In a wild place, there is a silent and richly layered energy that is palpable if you take a moment to feel it with your senses. Go to a wild place and listen with your body. Breathe and notice the quality of air compared to a cityscape. See the intricacies of shadow, light, color, and texture. Let your skin feel the sensations of exquisite coolness in such a place, and notice how your body becomes aware of an ancient knowing as you attune with this wild. Sense this pulse around you, a current of deep aliveness. This is the channel of the creative essence that moves through all living things.

We are a part of this flow, but we may hardly recognize this current within when we hurry along in the linear quest that defines our modern lifestyle. The wild holds medicine for the whole community with which we realign ourselves. Attuning with the wild, we reorient ourselves and make structures that incorporate this creative channel as the central flow. Making a life from this place is akin to returning to a natural spring and building our community there instead of heading off to the desert and spending all our time in search of water. Being in the wild provides a natural attunement of your energy field: aligning and nourishing your energy and bringing you back to your core and the knowing of what matters most. This poem by David Wagoner says it well:

> **Lost**
> *Stand still. The trees ahead and bushes beside you*
> *Are not lost. Wherever you are is called Here,*
> *And you must treat it as a powerful stranger,*
> *Must ask permission to know it and be known.*
> *The forest breathes. Listen. It answers,*
> *I have made this place around you.*
> *If you leave it, you may come back again, saying Here.*
> *No two trees are the same to Raven.*
> *No two branches are the same to Wren.*
> *If what a tree or a bush does is lost on you,*
> *You are surely lost. Stand still. The forest knows*
> *Where you are. You must let it find you.*[15]

If you don't have time to go to a wild place, take a walk outside, gaze at the sky, or move your work out into the sunshine. Put your feet onto the earth. Notice your energy field before and after you spend time with the earth's energy. Simple daily doses of earth medicine do wonders for your energy field and well-being. Touching the earth without shoes allows the pent-up energy charge from electronics to release down into the ground. The next time you use a computer for an extended period, take a break to touch the earth with bare or sock-covered feet, and feel the release from your body as you discharge the excess energy (this is an old cure for insomnia). This is a way to ground your energy field and clear the charge from your body that builds up from using the electronic devices that are increasingly a part of our lives.

There is earth-spirit medicine in the next exercise: a ritual of water blessing from traditional healer Rosita Arvigo, based on the Maya tradition. The power of ritual is that it works at the spirit–body interface to heal that which is difficult to name. This ritual brings the wild essence of plants, water, and spirit together into a blessing akin to holy water—one that can clarify the energy around your body and home, restoring the radiance of your center so you can more easily go there.

Exercise: Making a Spiritual Bath

1. Fill a bowl with water. Gather some leaves or flowers, particularly from plants you are drawn to (aromatic herbs and roses are ideal). As you gather the plant material, say a prayer, asking in your own way for divine assistance. Place the flower petals or leaves into the water, one at a time. When you have finished, notice the beauty you have created in this bowl.

2. Using your hands, squeeze the plant material in the water while saying a prayer. Ask for healing, protection, inspiration, or a blessing—whatever you need. As Rosita says, in passing along the teachings of Maya healer Don Elijio, "Trust—with all your heart—that blessings will come to you." Notice the quality of the air or energy that surrounds you.

3. Leave the bowl outside for an hour to receive the earth blessings that create a natural alignment of energy flow.

4. Return to the bowl and squeeze the plant matter once more, with thanks and prayer. Place the plant matter on the ground; then clar-

ify your energy field by splashing water into the air around your body, like a bird taking a bath. Imagine the blessing of this water extending into your whole creative field, brightening all the energy that comes into or radiates from your center.

5. Continue to bless your home by sprinkling water around it. Clarify the energy field of each doorway and room. Sprinkle the blessing water around the energy fields of other family members (or invite them to splash themselves); include your animal companions as well. When you have finished, pour this blessing water onto the earth with gratitude. Notice the radiance of your blessed and tended energy field.

Be Where You Are

The ability to be where you are, present in this central place with yourself, is essential for tracking your creative energy movement and the power of the moment. Being present in my center is the only way I am able to be abundantly creative in managing a multitude of regions in my life: mother, writer, healer, entrepreneur, partner, and homemaker. Rather than attempting to be creative in all areas at once, I follow the creative flow to the priority at hand. If I tried to make a list of everything I did, crossing off tasks in a linear manner, I would accomplish much less and with less creative insight. Instead, I live each day from the presence of my center and take direction from the guidance that arises naturally.

Maintaining presence in your center means having the willingness to acknowledge the challenging feelings that arise amid the energizing ones. If I wake up feeling overwhelmed, off kilter, or lacking a clear flow in my creative center, I clean and organize the house and attend to my body. I take a walk, do a sauna, spend time free writing, create a ritual, or read something that inspires. Tending the center first—until you feel a flowing energy again—is the priority. Trying to be creative when there is no inner flow is truly futile. Your creative core is where your creative focus is meant to be until you feel a sense of lightness or alignment in the center—and that may lead to an unexpected insight or direction. Though it's natural to try to fix or solve a given situation when you feel off kilter or when you encounter difficulty, pausing and receiving guidance from within is the way to align with your creative channel. Sometimes a person's best creative periods arise after a period of stagnation, as if the process of clearing the way allows for a new wave of energy to come in.

At other times, you may feel a bright current of energy that you can direct based on the inspiration that comes with it. I had an experience like this prior to the publication of my second book. In the back of my mind, I had been thinking about a book trailer for a year; but when the full picture of how it would look came in a flash, I wrote the text of the video in about fifteen minutes. I contacted a videographer the next day and planned for production when he returned from a trip. The day he was back in his office happened to be clear and bright; and responding to a feeling of excitement in my center, I asked if he wanted to shoot the outdoor video that afternoon. Though it required a rapid turnaround for both of us—him to shoot the video, and my husband and I to pick kids up from school and spontaneously take them to a video shoot (with snacks and fresh clothes and a pep talk about working together)—we said yes to the surge of energy.

We shot film for an hour and captured the magical energy of an inspired day that aligned perfectly with the beauty of my family. It felt almost too good to be true, yet that is the potential of aligning your actions with a creative surge. When you follow the creative flow, insights can become fully formed creations, creative projects can be rapidly fired into form, and obstacles can reveal new paths. Had I not been in touch with the energy current, I could have dismissed the impulse and decided there were too many factors to align in gathering three children and conveying my vision to the videographer. But by following the flow, we all came together: my family, the videographer, and me. Together, we stepped into the field of potential and recorded the vision I had already seen.

It rained the next day, and for weeks afterward.

Sense the Energy of the Day

At any given time, you may have several creative projects percolating or several directions calling to you, in addition to your other commitments. From the guidance of your center, note the top priorities that come to your attention and address them first. Sometimes they are in alignment with your to-do list; at other times, spontaneous activities may appear that you can incorporate without hesitation because they harmonize with the overall flow pattern.

To hone your creative edge, take the time to sense the essence of the day. From the center, ask yourself: *Is this a day for a creative project or running errands? Does the day have an open-ended quality or a more focused task orientation? Is this a day for family or business infrastructure, or both? Is something else rising to the forefront? Is self-care a priority?* In that way, tasks are accomplished by following the creative flow and guidance of the now, the present. Sometimes the creative priority is to address a personal need (including the need for fun) before having the creative space to be able to work. You may have a project that needs attention but wait until you feel from your center that it is time to turn your focus there. Being present in the center allows you to navigate an organic pathway through what otherwise would be overwhelming. Simply follow the flow.

Learning how to feel the flow of energy through your center in a given moment maximizes creative efficiency. It assists you in knowing when to say no to a project that does not resonate in your center—either because it is not quite aligned with your creative intentions or because it is simply not the right time for it. Then you are ready to step fully into a yes when you sense the energy building within. Creative direction and creative timing are less mental decisions than a practice of trusting this inner awareness. Ultimately, following the flow from the center aligns the whole creative field and the energy for each creation.

Where is your creative focus?
Is that in alignment with your center? If not, how can you realign with
   this place?

Savor the Moment

One morning, I was rushing off to work at my office. I had many things to do, but knowing that I wanted to carry a sense of inner stillness with me, I made an intentional pause. I stopped at the car door and, instead of driving off, turned to see the gold-tinged clouds lining the sky. Bare winter branches were moving in the cold wind; I felt my own breath. A line of geese traveled across the horizon. Then a blue heron flew low, right over my head—like a quiet blessing of the wild over the urban landscape.

I let myself sink into the spaciousness of the moment in order to see what was there: the slow up-and-down beat of the blue heron's wings, the open sky before me, the potential of the day. It is in moments like these intentional pauses that I make a practice of inhabiting where I am. I take root in the place where I reside and sense into the longings of my heart. I pause, take note of my senses, then begin to move again.

Slowly, I turned away from the winter sky and climbed into my car, carrying the quiet with me.

Being where you are ensures that you align with the energy of the moment to receive what it contains. These moments connect to the creative path of your soul over time. *Are you creative?* Live into the answer. Live into the unique expression coming through you. Live into a life made moment by moment and defined by the vast creative range of your heart.

FOUR

Cultivating Your Daily Creative Practice

Whatever you can do or dream you can do, begin it.
Boldness has genius, power, and magic in it. Begin it now.

—GOETHE

William Stafford was an acclaimed poet laureate and prolific writer from Oregon. He achieved success, but perhaps more intriguing was his devotion to a practice of writing every day early in the morning, while the rest of his household slept. He would arise in the dark before sunrise and then write, recording what came to the page, never missing a day. Over a period of fifty years, this daily habit of writing produced twenty thousand pages of writing and poetry, three thousand published poems, and eighty-five books of prose and poetry. Sometimes his writing was a series of musings; other times, brilliance that he shaped into poems like this one, "You Reading This, Be Ready," from his book *The Way It Is*:

> *Starting here, what do you want to remember?*
> *How sunlight creeps along a shining floor?*
> *What scent of old wood hovers, what softened*
> *sound from outside fills the air?*

Will you ever bring a better gift for the world
than the breathing respect that you carry
wherever you go right now? Are you waiting
for time to show you some better thoughts?

When you turn around, starting here, lift this
new glimpse that you found; carry into evening
all that you want from this day. This interval you spent
reading or hearing this, keep it for life—
What can anyone give you greater than now,
starting here, right in this room, when you turn around?[16]

William Stafford shaped his living habits around his creativity, and this current of creative energy was deeply defining of his life. He wrote the above poem two days before he died. It is so beloved that it was inscribed on a stone column near Lake Oswego, where he lived. Live a life with creativity as a practice, and creative energy will give expression to that life.

How to Make a Creative Practice

Creativity begins with an impulse, but it is practice that hones the form. Having a creative practice makes the time, space, and energy—a routine over time—that is necessary to formulate a creation. Making creativity a routine practice can assist you in overcoming resistance to your creative impulses. Rather than becoming bogged down in trying to create something specific or achieve a certain outcome, simply begin the practice and engage the energy that arrives. Take the photo, write the sentence, move the body, sing the note, press the piano key, moisten the paintbrush, plant the seed; begin.

There are two essential aspects of establishing a creative practice: *form* and *inspiration*. You need a form, the physical components of a regular space and time, to practice your art. Then you need the inspiration that moves your creative spirit. For William Stafford, writing was his inspiration, so he made a form to engage it by writing for a set time each morning. The spirit of creativity is enhanced when we make routine time for it; the creative channel is stronger when we value its flow.

Ponder your own creative form. What is the best time of day for you creatively: morning, afternoon, night? Where will you create—at home, in an office, at a cafe, in an open space, with other people, alone? When can you make time to be creative that will fit into your schedule, or how can you shift your schedule to make time? Do you have a creative space or can you make one for yourself? What do you need in order to make creative time for yourself—focus, clear commitment, childcare, a change in schedule, a place?

Once you have a concept of the form for your creative practice, ponder the inspiration. What type of creative practice inspires you—dance, writing, visual art, nature, daydreaming, spending time with children, music, gardening, cooking? When are you most inspired each day, each week, each season? I prefer to write on Tuesdays, for example, so I schedule my healing practice with women on Wednesdays and Thursdays. I find that certain days have a rhythm that influences what I'm inspired to do. Similarly, I teach in fall and spring because of the outward energy moving me at that time. Then I retreat with my family and personal creative practice in the summer and winter.

Where are you most inspired—a quiet room, the kitchen, a noisy bar, outside? What landscape inspires you—urban, forest, river, mountain, field, ocean, tended garden, wild nature? What do you need in order to be more inspired—time in the wild, an art class, a hands-on activity, the company of friends or community, a new environment, less stress, coffee? What happens when you are inspired? How do you feel in your body: sad, sleepy, ecstatic, like you want to yell, cry, laugh, sing?

A creative practice is made up of form and inspiration, and many artists intuitively create a body of work this way. We can look to an artist like William Stafford, who saw art as a way to live more richly, to inspire our creative practice regardless of whether we are creating art or just living creatively. Creative energy makes a bountiful life and opens us to new ways of being.

Dream Seeds: My Most Essential Creative Practice

Working with the body–energy interface, I am intrigued by patterns that give shape to energy within and around us. I am particularly interested in aligning these inner and outer patterns to enhance creative flow. Astrology examines these patterns through the influence and movement of planets. When you understand the astrology mapping that influences your birth-energy field, you can discover the abilities or tools you have for addressing common challenges you may encounter.

To this end, my most essential creative practice for making a form to enhance creativity is based on a yearly process of setting intentions. I look forward to this annual ritual the way a gardener thumbs through winter seed catalogs, planning out the plantings for spring. This practice comes from a powerful little book that entered my life more than a decade and a half ago: *The Book of Houses* by Robert Cole and Paul Williams, two men in touch with their feminine fields who invite the reader to select a set of creative intentions to focus on as a harvest cycle over a full year's time.

When I found this book, I was in search of something undefined. Having completed my graduate studies in physical therapy, I was working my first professional job. Pursuing this long career trajectory had pulled me away from my own sense of desire. I felt restless, as if something was missing, but did not know where to begin to find or reclaim it. The book contains a simple plan for cultivating one's own creative intentions for the year—or "dream seeds," as the authors name them. Based on one's personal astrology, the book guides the reader through a process of paying attention to the monthly rhythms that influence dream-seed cultivation. The authors help the reader determine how their astrological chart corresponds to a year's passage, pairing their personal astrological chart with the twelve houses that make up themes of energy movement over the course of a year. Since we are each born at different points during the year, our own harvest cycle is unique. I can attest to the power of tending to one's creative harvest over time and through the seasons of energy.

The influence of greater energy cycles interacting with our own energy fields will affect our creative capacity throughout the year, but we can engage these rhythms in intentional ways. Regardless of whether you follow the influences of astrology or not, it is a vital creative practice to set yearly intentions and revisit them each month to bring consciousness to cultivating your creative energy. Use Cole and Williams's book to find out your "intention-setting time," or choose a time for yourself to make a list of five to seven creative goals that address all the major areas of your life: home, work, partnerships, children, creative projects or outlets, health, daily life. Learning how to work with seasonal energy for cultivating creative intentions is powerful creative medicine. Do this practice over one year, and you will witness new patterns and creations in your life as a result.[17]

There is power in simply formulating specific intentions on the page, because putting your intentions into words requires that you take your insights and give them defined form. Then make time to review these intentions regularly, such as at the beginning of each month, or on the full or new moon; choose a time that will remind you to engage this practice as a routine. After one year of monthly reflections, study these dream seeds to assess how your intentions matched your creative direction and the manifestation of your dreams. Think about how you would like to refocus your energy, and then write a new set of five to seven goals for the next year.

In setting annual creative goals for myself, I've included such past intentions as these: outline a book, speak at two new workshop venues, establish new online forms for classes, find opportunities for spontaneous play and adventure with my children, have dates with my husband, take three family trips to different landscapes, make smoothies for daily vitality. Notice how the goals/dream seeds include my family as equal to my work, and focus on nurturing my marriage and personal health. I check my dream seeds at least once a month by rereading them during a quiet evening, to keep them fresh in my mind through the year. I let my actions for specific cultivation—such as when to plant versus when to leave an area fallow—be guided by the seasonal influence. In this process, I find that I am intensely productive but also creatively fulfilled and in contact with my dreams.

By setting clear intentions, I'm ready when an opportunity arises that matches something on my list; I can step into it without hesitation. Take, for example, the year I had set an intention to find a larger office space. This intention came to me as an inspiration when I was reflecting on the previous year. Until it came into my mind, I did not even realize it was something I desired. I wrote it down as an intention, thinking it might be a few years before I would actually change spaces. About six months later, though, I heard that one of my office mates in a two-room suite was moving out of the building. I quickly contacted the landlord to express interest in this larger space. One year later, I found myself moved in and enjoying the extra room and light-filled windows. Though it is a rare combination in today's world, engaging the internal realm first before taking action—in order to chart your life—is a model for the future.

At the end of the year, reflect on which of your creative goals came to fruition, taking note of where your focus was, and then write new goals to continue weaving this creative thread. Keep them in one place so you can look back year after year to see how your ability to focus your dreams evolves over time. Some items will be visible creations that have come into form like works of art, but some will be the infrastructure to hold these creations, such as work and personal schedules; class outlines and details; business practices; networking plans; personal spirit, body, and energy work; and vacations and intentional pauses to refill the well. The cycles will continue as cycles do—through the seasons, over the years—becoming the richly layered aspects of a creative life.

Pair Creative Flow with Creative Goals

In addition to annual creative goals, establish routine activities that match these goals and inspire your day-to-day creativity. While you keep your overall goals in mind, notice how your creative center responds to the way you direct your creative energy. This allows you to pair creative flow with creative goals. Goal setting is the more masculine aspect, often overdeveloped in a production-oriented society; the flow is the feminine aspect and actually comes first, both to shape the goals and then to guide the creative rhythm for when and how to work on them.

If you feel energized and inspired, you are moving in alignment with your vitality. If you are feeling frustrated or depleted, reidentify your creative priorities to ensure that they are in sync with your creative energy and desires. Again, it is essential to balance the two aspects of a creative practice: inspiration and form.

One simple way I inspire my creative energy is through writing, so I write every day, whether it is a section for a book, blog post, class outline, free-form creative thought, or journal page. It's all too easy for our focus to become consumed by the idea of "getting things done"—forgetting that one is never "done"—and lose touch with the abundant and infinite creative essence. Regular practice of something that inspires us helps us stay connected to our creative-currency flow in tangible and daily ways.

Starting every morning with a brief energy-sensing meditation (like the "Exploring Your Creative-Energy Field" exercise on page 39) will allow you to ponder the state of your inner landscape, the direction of your creative energy, and the beauty outside your window that reveals the timeless flow happening in nature all around. Once this femi-nine connection to your energy is established, it's easier to engage the flow in your daily routines. Rather than thinking about the myriad of tasks yet to be accomplished, focus on being purely present with your breath, your body, the wild within, and the sensations of moving in the present moment.

Another simple way to stay in contact with the inspirational aspect of creative flow is to notice and embody your creative practice by attending with all senses to what you feel, see, hear, and intuit. When the opportunity arises to give your attention to whatever is most important to you, practice prioritizing the present moment by dropping whatever else you are doing and offering it your full attention. Though the phrase "be in the moment" has been overused to the point of cliché, these embodied moments are what give us energy. Let yourself be inspired by what the moment contains. A practice of daily tending with presence fills your deepest creative wells so you can draw from their potential.

On the other hand, if you are moving with the flow of your life without setting clear intentions, you may not be directing your mascu-line creative aspect with clarity. Too much inspiration without form is an imbalance that will affect what you create. In fact, though the mas-culine *doing* aspect tends to be overly developed in a culture focused on production, when you harness it for yourself, it becomes an essential component of giving form to your dreams. Aligning creative flow with creative goals means using both the feminine inspiration and the mas-culine framework with intention.

Energy Session: Embodying the Feminine, Re-engaging the Masculine

When Seth came for an energy session, he found that his professional life and his romantic life were not moving forward the way he desired. He was working as a teacher but felt there was more of himself that he wanted to express. In his personal life, he found that his relationships with women so far had not inspired him. Though women were attracted to him, he had not yet had a relationship that engaged his full attraction. When he was talking about this, I noticed that the left aspect of his energy field—the feminine aspect—was undefined, as if he did not fully inhabit it. This type of pattern, in a male or a female, will tend to draw unwanted attention from others without allowing the individual to cultivate a clear focus on what they actually desire to attract.

Seth's right energy field and masculine aspect, while more defined, was hardly engaged. Again, he was reacting to life (both in regard to work and relationships) rather than dynamically creating what he wanted; and his energy field reflected both this pattern and the antidote for change. Rather than focusing on redefining his work or how to find a partner, I invited him to reflect on his own energy field.

First I asked Seth to sense into both the left and right aspects of his energy by looking with his inner eye and feeling with his inner sense. He noted that he could feel the left side more than the right side but concurred that the left felt more open, as if it had no boundary. I suggested he walk along the left half of his energy field in his mind's eye to increase his awareness of the edge of his creative-energy field. For most people, there is a habitual way of inhabiting the energy field that they are not even aware of. It requires working with more subtle awareness to notice the pattern and then changing it by interacting with the energy through visualization, focused breathing, or energy-sensing meditations.

The openness on Seth's left side attracted energy, but since he was less present there, he wasn't sending clear signals about what he wanted to attract. To create what we want in any aspect of our lives, it is helpful to embody the left, feminine field of attraction so that what we draw is in alignment with our energy. Then we can use the masculine field of direction to actively generate and create with the energy we've drawn in.

Once Seth had a more defined boundary on the left aspect of his field, I invited him to move into the sense of his right energy field and his capacity for directing his life. While doing so, I invited him to think about what he wanted to create in terms of a partner and work—more in the sense of the energy he desired to move toward rather than any specific details. For Seth to move out of the defensive mode of simply responding to unwanted energy or going through the motions at work, he had to instead open his energy to receive the feminine flow of inspiration. Receiving this energy for himself, he could then engage his dynamic masculine to set intentions and take steps toward the direction of his desires. Then it is back to the feminine for refined inspiration, and again to the masculine for actions that respond to the inspiration; the feminine and masculine within are meant to engage in partnership. But this alignment begins first in one's own energy field. By inhabiting the two aspects of his whole creative field, Seth could establish an inner energy alignment to further manifest as dynamic forms and relationships in his outer life.

Exercise: Choosing Creative Intentions and Dream Seeds

Find a quiet place, a pad of paper, and a pen.

1. Begin by listing five to seven creative goals or dream seeds for the year. Make sure they cover the many aspects of your life, including home, partnership, work, health, creative dreams, and so on.
2. When you have the overall goals identified, flesh them out fully to be as specific and as clear as possible.
3. Now make a list of daily ways to inspire your creativity. List whatever comes to mind and the ways in which you are currently finding creative expression.
4. Compare your overall goals and your daily creative practice. Are your daily activities based on obligations or do they represent the way you truly want to spend your time and energy? Are the ways

you know to engage your creativity in sync with your overall goals? Where are they clearly in alignment, and where might you fine-tune your daily practice or overall goals to be more intentional with your creative energy? How does your time spent in a day match these goals and practices? How might you shift your focus to enhance your creative flow?

5. Refine your two lists as needed, then keep them close at hand so you can check them once a week. This will ensure that you are using your creative energy as a daily practice that routinely syncs with the grand direction of your creative goals.

Define Your Creative Space

Creativity carries the energy of inspiration, but the energy needs a solid container to generate, hold, and sustain it. As we become more connected through computers, without the previous boundaries of defined schedules, it is more essential to establish creative spaces by dedicating specific time to focus your energy. The experience of immersing oneself in the creative wellspring typically requires a few hours of uninterrupted time. This means securing and committing to such time, as this is where the fluid nature of creativity still needs the form of clear intention and focus. Guarding this creative space involves turning off potential distractions, such as email or the web, in order to make a window for being creative.

Once you have time, organize the place where you will be working so you are free to create. Clear away any clutter and distractions, and let yourself be in the creative space. If I plan to spend several hours writing, the first task on my list is to have a clear desk. I take care of any immediate needs—any directions arising from my center that may come spontaneously—and then I clear the dishes and the table where I will be working so the creative movement can begin. Only after clarifying the space do I start to write. Since it is possible to do so many things that no time is left for the actual creating, I limit the organizing process to a certain period of time. But preparing the space is part of making room for creative inspiration.

Tending the space around your creative practice means balancing creativity with taking care of daily life. Cleaning the house, preparing food, raking leaves, walking the dog, playing with the children, and other aspects of maintenance keep you grounded throughout the creative process. Working with creative energy puts you in a frame of mind where time and space are fluid. This realm of spirit and passion can inspire the body but also deplete it if you lose touch with the ground. Rather than diminishing creativity, the simple caretaking tasks in daily life that invite breaks actually strengthen the container that holds your creative energy.

Is your creative space defined, or how would you like it to be?
How are you making time and space to contain a creative flow?

Prioritize Your Creativity

Since daily tasks can crowd out creative time, finding time for creativity means that it has to be one of your priorities. There are many ways to use creative energy, but generally, it should be something hands-on that involves crafting or shaping an energy flow, and that is ideally done every day, or at least on a routine basis. Making creativity routine is what hones your practice and your ability to access your full creative capacity.

The other aspect of prioritizing and developing creative potential is maintaining focus in two to three creative directions. Rather than dispersing creative energy across many areas, simply returning to the same ground again and again will build a tangible product from your creative efforts over time. It can take years to hone a craft, and it requires both discipline and focus. Whether you are becoming a musician, a skilled writer, a master gardener, a successful professional, or the master creator of your dreams, the same thing is required: routine daily effort over a period of at least a decade.

Limiting your focus to a few aspects of creativity does not diminish your creative current; it deepens it. Similar to an artist who spends decades crafting a form to a high art, choosing a specific form to practice helps hone creative essence—and all aspects of creativity—and your own being receives the benefits of creative mastery that arise from practice.

Another way to focus yourself is to write a personal mission statement, the way businesses do, to clarify your priorities for your creative essence. Mine is this: *To meet spirit in a daily way—while raising children; making a home; engaging my partner; working with the ancient energy in the body, as a creative being and within my own center—as nourishment, expression, and celebration of this life*. Ponder your own creative mission.

> *How do you integrate creative flow with the tasks of daily life?*
> *What are your top three creative fires, or what would you like them to be?*
> *What is your personal creative mission statement?*

Know What Makes You Feel Creative

If you know what makes you feel creative and how you like to be in touch with your creative energy, you are more likely to make time for it and engage it spontaneously. If you don't know how to access your creative energy, the challenge is to experiment creatively until you find your inspiration. This is when going into the wild can help you tune in to and hear your inner creative voice.

The wild offers limitless creative inspiration. For example, I have watched the constrained play of children on playgrounds—particularly on today's formulated plastic playgrounds that are often almost identical from one park to another—compared to the expansive and limitless play that occurs in a wild place. My favorite place is the ocean, where my children's play is inspired by the offerings of the sea; but even the trails in a park invite more creativity in all of us. Nature's infinite forms inspire creative play; going into nature replenishes and inspires the creative well. Thus, everyone needs an access point for routine contact with this inner spaciousness. Touching the limitless forms in nature or in the wild within nurtures wholeness and reignites creative passions.

What makes you feel creative or inspires you to create?
How are structure and wildness related to your creativity?

Energy Session: Feeling Creative Is Essential for Being Creative

Gina came for a session to receive clarity about her creative purpose. A student in a stressful graduate program where she had difficulty standing out, she found herself making comparisons to her sister, a successful artist who seemed to live visibly and glamorously. Gina longed for that type of connection to her creativity and vibrance. I asked her where she felt in touch with her creativity, and she had to think about it. Mostly, she was feeling uncreative and frustrated about it without doing anything to change it. She also focused much of her attention on working hard at school and looking to her professors for validation; she noted her tendency to look to others for security and approval. In reflecting on the overview of her life, Gina realized how much she needed a visible expression of her own creative spark.

While it would be difficult for Gina to engage her creativity while being fully immersed in school, the primary change to make was in regard to her inner feeling state. Becoming aware of a deficiency can guide actions for change, but simply bemoaning the deficit will only reinforce the current pattern. No one else can change that internal sense that something is lacking; not our professors, employers, partners, friends, or family. Only we ourselves can move energy from a sense of lack to one of being fulfilled.

I invited Gina to envision herself being creative, first by remembering a sense of it in her body. Bringing her attention to her center and imagining creativity, the first image that came to her mind was of horseback riding and the freedom she felt as a girl when riding. Her family owned a small farm and two horses, one of whom was her constant companion. Gina had ridden in the surrounding hillsides throughout her childhood and young-adult years. In this moment, she saw that, for her, creativity was a feeling of freedom—particularly freedom in motion—which she didn't have presently.

I asked Gina if she knew of a place where she could start riding horses again. She replied that there was a farm offering lessons about thirty minutes from her home. She had planned to look into it but put it off because of her hectic school schedule. She would still need to evaluate the stables and see about the care of the horses, but now she recognized the freedom of riding as something essential to her core self. Rekindling the feeling of creativity was a direct move toward nourishing her creative essence.

Gina and I talked further about how creativity is more than the act of making art or being validated by one's creations, but rather a sense of one's connection to life and potential. Now Gina had a vision of what she was truly looking for. Beyond striving for the picture she held of her sister's life or waiting for her graduate program to provide her with sustenance, Gina could bring a sense of creative vibrance directly into her life.

Feeling creative is essential for being creative. To be able to create something requires a flow of creative energy or currency. And there are many ways to tap into one's creative currency, often unique to each person. Establishing an ample flow of creative currency is the first step toward generating its tangible expression.

Live in the Flow

Beyond simply accessing your creative flow part-time, it is possible to live in the flow. Living in the flow expands the potency of your creative currency for building wealth in your life; it allows you to tap into the broader energy current that infuses your cells with chi, or life energy. One of my closest friends finds her creative essence in her garden, whether tending to her plants, eating from their bounty, or enjoying their beauty around her home. While working in the garden feels like a chore to me, it aligns her center and helps her orient to what is important. The effect of working in the garden is visible in her bright face, her light tone, and the ease of her movements. All of her energy moves more serenely into her life after a morning gardening session. Though gardening is unrelated to her work, it has everything to do with manifesting her creative energy. Likewise, the beauty and alignment of the well-tended garden that surrounds her home continues to nurture her as she moves into the rest of her day.

When you are in the creative flow, you will find an expansive sense that anything is possible. This state of inhabiting the possibility of everything is the opposite of the critical mind that tends to question every minute detail. Runners talk about this as the "runner's high"; spiritual seekers describe it as unity or ecstasy; visionaries dream of the full realm of possibilities during these times. This is the feminine capacity for pure visioning and awe-filled inspiration. It is the ability to inhabit the present moment and create from that pure presence. An example of someone who does this is Naomi Pomeroy, the talented young chef and owner of Beast restaurant in Portland, Oregon. She designs her restaurant's four-course menu each week based on what she finds at the farmers' market. What sets Pomeroy apart is her willingness to work in the present flow, inventing recipes on the spot as the fresh ingredients inspire her.

In addition to tapping creative flow, visionaries need either the masculine skills of strategic form and focus or the presence of more detail-oriented people around them to execute dreams on the ground. The masculine skill set enables one to capitalize on feminine inspiration and sort through the details of how something may be accomplished.

If the feminine and masculine are in good relationship, the feminine inspiration comes in and the masculine form is made. If, however, the masculine arises first and the feminine essence is not allowed to take shape freely, the critical and detailed perspective of the masculine is louder than the expansive dreamer, disrupting broader creative expression before we can even ponder our full potential.

In this same manner, the realities of tending to everyday life may not seem to relate to the expansiveness of creative dreams. Creative insights can arise as sudden inspiration but may not sync with your agenda, which is already filled with tasks to accomplish for the day. When I receive a creative impulse that has workshop or writing potential, I quickly write it down in note form on a piece of paper. I want to capture that expansive creative essence that is beneath many of the best ideas and breakthroughs. Then I tuck the paper into a file to be explored more fully when I have time to be actively creative. In this way, I am able to capture threads of insight that might otherwise be lost; I provide a place for my creativity (and my dreamy feminine inspirations) to land and then make the time to work with these insights later (with my focused masculine energy). Or if I am working on a creative project but feel as if I am becoming mired in the details, I will take a walk outside or spend time meditating to restore a broader creative bandwidth, infusing the details with more energy.

Patterns of creativity, both daily rhythms and the overall creative journey, move through periods of outward expansion and creative visibility that alternate with periods of restoration and retreat. Creativity mirrors the natural movement of seasonal life-force energy; the quiet season of winter renewal (and more dormant creative periods) is as essential as the blossoms of spring or the fruit of summer (when creativity is flowing outwardly and creative projects are more visible). Understanding these patterns and how to work with them daily and seasonally allows for greater cultivation and realization of a thriving creative practice, because it naturally tends the creative field.

Being able to facilitate feminine inspiration with masculine structure or focus while attending to the greater patterns of flow and form
is an art in itself. Using the expansive feminine and focused masculine
capacities together will enable you to weave your inspirations into a
particular form—a book, a dance, or a moment of expression—but
also to thread it into the many realms of living. In doing so, your life
takes on the shimmer of your creative passion.

What practices or people connect you to a sense of possibility?
What would you do if you felt anything was possible? How does this
    relate to your dreams?

Energy Session: What Are You Waiting For?

Lila came for a session to re-energize her center because she felt creatively stagnant and was not sure about the root cause of this feeling.
As we began the session, I placed my hands over her pelvic bowl, and
the first question that came to mind was *What are you waiting for?* As
an energy reader, I often translate the wisdom of what a person's body
or energy field would convey to them if they were listening. Most of
us have learned to listen to the sources outside of ourselves more than
our own centers, and so give authority to the outer world instead of listening to the inner one. I relayed this question to Lila and, as wisdom
from a person's core often does, it rang true for her.

In this moment of listening, Lila recognized that she was placing
her creative potential on hold until she had an established career and a
committed relationship. It was as if she were waiting until her life felt
more secure to exercise her creativity. Instead of living in her creative
center, she was waiting for her life to reach certain milestones. Yet her
creative essence was vital right then for building the life she desired. Lila
knew this to be true, and she saw how she unconsciously ignored her creative impulses—as if they would only be available once she had achieved
a certain "level of success" (a particular income or status of recognition).

In bringing this awareness to her conscious mind, she could engage it with more intention. Instead of placing her creative dreams and desires on hold while she set up her life, she could engage them as a part of the process of building her life with passion and creativity at the center.

I asked how her life would be different if she were engaging her creativity right now. She answered with a string of ideas: take more risks socially and accept invitations to go out, have spontaneous fun, attend a dance class that captured her attention, reimagine her sense of style, try kayaking, stop striving, and enjoy where she is now. By listening to her center, Lila found many immediate and simple ways to engage her creativity.

Life is happening right now, and the creative current has relevance for you. There is no pinnacle to reach before you can access your creative potential. Creative essence is developed by using it daily, and it thrives when you bring it to life. Contacting your creative currency on a routine basis gives room for your expression and inspires the direction for your life as one seamless flow. But having a vibrant life requires a strong creative current to bring forth the vibrance. Lila rediscovered that a creative path lay right in front of her and laughed out loud: "What am I waiting for?" The time—and the life—is now.

Tapping Into the Power of Inner Vision

Another way to live in the flow of your creative field is to hone the power of visualization. Just like athletes who visualize optimal performance prior to competition, you can visualize with intention to engage your full energy capacity. Mike Dooley, author of *Manifesting Change*, recommends imagining your creative goals as already having been completed. Instead of thinking about "how" you are going to do something—which tends to engage the critical mind more than the energy field of pure potential, interfering with creativity—simply envision your dreams as fully realized. Dooley recommends visualizing while feeling a strong sense of satisfaction or celebration. Since our feelings are powerful, we often focus too intensely on the negative or difficult feelings rather than the expansive joy or gratitude that will better energize the creative field. Top athletes do not question whether they can accomplish something, nor do they seek permission from others—they dream it, feel it, live it. If you aren't sure about what your vision is for yourself, go back to the exercise about choosing dream seeds and start from there (see "Choosing Creative Intentions and Dream Seeds" on page 120). Remember that dreams are like gardens, in that they manifest abundance through long-term, focused tending.

Wayne Gretzky, the greatest hockey player who has ever lived, started dreaming about playing hockey when he was just a boy; but he is especially fascinating because, as one of the smallest players, he was mocked at first. Rather than listening to the naysayers, Gretzky changed the sport of hockey—and beliefs about who could play—just by adding his unique form to it. While other players slammed into one another and made plays through aggression and force, he scored by being wildly creative. He played all shooting angles, including bouncing pucks off other players; he created new moves and ways of working with teammates to assist one another; he scored a record number of goals but also a record number of assists. No one had ever played hockey like he did. Gretzky said that when he played, everything moved in slow motion—that is how present he was in the pure flow.

Exercise: Visualizing Your Potential

Many gifted athletes describe playing or moving in a zone like the one Gretzky describes—the zone of pure potential that we can all draw energy from. To develop this potential, it is helpful to spend time sensing, visualizing, or otherwise energizing your connection to the greater energy field. The following exercise can assist in this process:

1. Begin this exercise by pondering three of your most expansive creative dreams; for example, writing in a mountain cabin, traveling

around the world, finding your soul mate, taking your family to live in another country, meeting a great visionary, making a huge personal leap, or starting a business that truly excites you.

2. Give your imagination permission to expand to the greatest dreams you can imagine. Too often we limit our imagination to what we "think" is possible; or we live in the day-to-day reality and forget to dream expansively. When you free your imagination to dream, you are tapping into the potential of energy that has no limitations. It means seeing yourself in the dreams of your heart and giving more range to your creative desires.

3. Notice where you tend to limit yourself and where you allow yourself to expand your dreams (remember to imagine your dreams fully realized, already complete and real). Notice the sensations or feelings you have while envisioning your dreams. Feel the expanse of your energy field, and take note of what you receive in this expansive form.

4. Ask what you need in order to receive or step into this vision. Is there an action to take, a limitation to release, an opening to allow, or some other guidance? Can you remember the feeling of possibility in your center?

5. When this exercise feels complete, give thanks for these visions. Then close by promising to take steps each day in the direction of building and receiving your dreams.

Bring Your Dreams to Life

The challenging aspect of making a creative life is formulating the practical aspects of living while incorporating your dreams into the process. The very nature of dreams—their expansiveness and fluid quality—makes them essential for envisioning creative potential, but it generally sends you in the opposite direction from what is required for managing the details of living. Again, the busyness of simply making a living or taking care of the home can lead you off course from what you truly want or dream for yourself. It is vital to know the call within your soul even within the daily details—to be able to steer your life force in the direction of this call. Take a moment to list on a piece of paper the most expansive creative dreams you imagined in the last exercise, or do that exercise now. When you finish, keep this paper close by, perhaps with your dream seeds (see page 120), so that your dreams and creative intentions remain near the actual life you are making.

Becoming a creative master means learning how to align the bird's-eye view of your most expansive creative dreams with the on-the-ground focus of day-to-day creativity. You need both the daily inspiration (which connects you to your creative energy) and the overall creative vision (which directs this flow) in order to achieve your dreams. Once you have clear ideas about how to routinely access your creative essence, call to mind your broader vision—the dream seeds that guide your creative intentions. Keep your routine creative focus on the day-to-day flow, but maintain an awareness of your creative dreams; they are the overall map and direction for where you are heading.

Energy Session: Dreaming with Intention

When Mary came to see me, she was the picture of a woman who had it all: a mother, homemaker, and successful part-time executive. Though she felt engaged, she also felt scattered; she was busy yet unfulfilled. When I asked about her greatest creative dreams—what she wanted for herself as a creative being—she did not know how to answer.

In our session, I invited her to let herself dream whatever she could imagine for herself and her family, to liberate her creative essence and move in the direction of her dreams. When she did this, instead of a bright energy pattern, the energy in her center took on a contracted quality—because the creative energy was clearly not flowing. I asked what was happening for her. She opened her eyes and said that she would start to dream but then worry about how this detail or that detail could possibly happen; she questioned herself on every aspect. And if she didn't question herself, she imagined that her husband would; she had even internalized the overly logical voice of her husband, a corporate lawyer with highly developed analytical skills, further emphasizing her pattern of questioning herself.

Mary had built her life around her family and work rather than any creative dream that arose purely from her center. Whenever someone cannot name their dreams, they have often built the structure of their life outside themselves, such as around their partner's desires, the demands of a career, or the needs of a family. Trying to connect with her dreams was a new exercise for Mary. Tuning back in to the dream space within can re-establish the creative currency that feeds the soul.

Besides designing her life around work and family, Mary was allowing her linear or logical mind to engage before her dreams could even take shape; she halted her creative inspiration before it had a chance to build into something tangible. I suggested to Mary that if she could not imagine her creative dreams in her center and allow them to take form, it would be difficult to manifest them in the physical world. Many successful athletes, musicians, and other performers first imagine and believe the potential for success exists before they can make it happen. If they do not believe in this potential, it will be difficult to achieve their goals. It is the same with creative energy. Allowing the vision to be created within sets its potential; then the flow guides it to manifestation. We do not have to know how to get there, but we have to believe the potential exists in order to gather the necessary energy for building our dreams. We must sense and feel our way into the potential; we must dream with intention before we can live our dreams.

When Mary returned to her center, the primary word that came to her in relation to her dreams was "love." I asked her to imagine what love might mean for her, since each person has a different way of experiencing this feeling. When she focused on the word *love*, nothing moved in the energy of her center. But when she began to visualize this word, she could see herself at her favorite mountain lake, boating and swimming with her family. She realized that as much as she wanted to give love to her family, she wanted to bask in and fully receive the love available in her life. She had been putting off a family trip because of various scheduling restraints. Now, instead of worrying about how she could take time off from work or how she could adjust her family schedule, she held the vision of her family at the lake resort. The energy of her center came to life. Starting with the vision and then moving into the details is an effective way to do this. Mary could feel the warmth emanating from her center as she began to allow the energy of her dreams to take root and guide the way.

The picture we create of our dreams does not have to be fully articulated; it just needs to carry the energy of what it feels like when our dreams are realized. When you are setting up a dream vision, it can be helpful to picture yourself doing something that makes you feel joyful and free, as sensations of joy and liberation are in sync with the realization of dreams. Mary focused on this expression for herself, giving herself permission to dream without trying to decipher the specifics of how her dreams might happen, and the energy became radiant and full in her center. This is the resonance or energy form of her dreams, and finding this resonance on a daily basis is the key to making them real. Feeling the resonance of this energy in her own center directs Mary to make family time a priority but also invites her to take more time for daily expressions of love, providing the structure and form with which she can realize her dreams.

Ground yourself solidly in the energy of your dreams to practice a state of being that will draw upon this potential. Envision your dreams in the creative-energy field and allow them to take shape in your imagination. Contemplate the essence of your dreams fully realized, then use your imagination to craft a form for each dream. Each one of us carries dream seeds within; life is not meant to draw us away from these seeds. Having a creative practice is the thread that sows these dream seeds into the fabric of our lives.

FIVE

Bringing Spirit into Form

Artists live in unknown spaces and give themselves over
to following something unknown.

—KIKI SMITH

One night, a friend asked me how I knew there was something more to this life than the here and now of what we can see in our physical reality. Hearing his words, I realized how different my life, at its core, was from his. Every day brings me in contact with the mystery and its pulse in the ordinary moments of living through the creative current in my center—because I make space for it in the center of my life.

In our culture, we are rarely in touch—in a daily way—with birth, death, and the creative cycles of living. Many of us are contained comfortably in the walls of our homes or work spaces, removed and potentially unable to feel a full sense of aliveness. I am blessed to work in the creative center of the body as a healer, dropping into the heart of people's longings, desires, losses, and creative essence where they give birth and life to their dreams. This practice keeps me in touch with something expansive that words can hardly contain. Whatever we choose to do, when we are able to sense this inner connection to the mystery, and even move with it, our personal creative expression becomes an intimate journey with spirit.

Keep Company with Spirit

Creativity is the process of taking spirit—in the form of an inspired notion—and giving it form. The movement of spirit into body is how we come into being. In recognizing the energy current that flows in your body, you return to the tangible or embodied awareness of spirit in your life. If you perceive the creative process as a sacred one, you see how creativity helps forge a connection with the divine. Delving into creativity is therefore a way to heal and restore the presence of spirit in one's body and life.

A friend of mine assists an annual tending of the "dragon kiln," an earthen kiln in the Coast Range of Oregon where a group of artists gather in a ritual process. They place their art pieces into the kiln, light the fire, and feed the wood-burning kiln all hours of the day and night for four to seven days. Prior to the lighting of the fire, the community of potters expresses the reflections, hopes, and intentions for each piece. They also honor the materials, such as local wood, and the other elements—wind, rain, spirit—that will affect the emergent process of the firing. Made of earth itself, the kiln is like a great womb large enough to hold all of the artworks and several people as they load it. Pieces are passed from person to person and then placed in the muffled quiet of the earthen walls. Before the loading began one day, I sat in the heart of the kiln with my friend and her daughter, and we all whispered like children in a secret cave, tracing patterns on bricks glaze-covered from the heat of decades of previous fires.

During the firing, flames sweep through the kiln, eddying and flowing around the pieces much like a river. The clay is transformed through the alchemical mixture of heat and fire, earth and spirit. When my friend tends the fire of the dragon kiln, she is in the presence of the mystery and transformative processes at work within and around the kiln. Placing carefully cut wood so the heat is sustained through each night, she keeps company with spirit. She tells me that opening the kiln after the firing is a sacred day, the objects still warm with the fire of transformation. Frequently, the results are surprising: vessels and other forms are changed beyond human intention. Whether the ceramics end up on the table as bowls for soup or on the altar as objects for other rituals, they hold the spirit of the fire, revivifying the home with the memory of creative integration.

The challenge of making art and engaging with spirit is that we have to make our way back into the physical world of both potential and limitation. After my initial foray into the publishing world, where my first book proposal was turned down by major publishing houses, I was left with a partially finished manuscript. I had received the creative inspiration but no form to contain it. As a mother, with my days spent taking care of my two young children, I felt that I could either abandon my creative project (and limit my capacity to encourage my children—with authenticity—to follow their dreams) or I could find a deeper reservoir to nourish my creative essence.

Crying out to spirit by the river in the story that opens this book, I received an answer to my call in the form of a personal encounter with an eagle. Rather than trying to find another form for my book project, I called more intently to spirit. Spirit gave me something in return: a sense of potential within. This encounter profoundly altered my sense of being in my body. A new energy connection was forged that led me in a new direction. In the days that followed this encounter, I received creative insight that formed the basis for a workshop that I would ultimately teach many times over several years. I called this workshop "Realigning with the Great Mother."

This next section includes the framework of the workshop and the information I discovered for keeping company with spirit. It is an energetic process designed to restore the sacredness of the creative current that is our birthright as uniquely creative beings. Think of it as a bridge to the creative field we are meant to live from. This framework, taught in a class format, brought insight and healing to the many women who

participated, but also to me as the teacher. It allowed me to further
repair my energy field, which held generations of imprinted disconnect
from the greater mysteries of energy. After this vital energy connection
was restored, I was able to receive guidance and sustenance from a
deeper creative current in order to write for several more years and
eventually self-publish my first book. This connection then continued
to guide my work and, to this day, informs our work–family dynamic
flow. May it serve to assist your creative journey as well.

To create is to risk failure. The job may not come through, the art
may not receive recognition, the pregnancy may not occur, or the relationship may not last. The musician's CD may not produce a hit or
achieve market success. My son is a talented musician, but at the age of
twelve, he began to question whether he could "make it" as a musician—
as if that were the only measure of success. I told him then (and continue
to tell all of my sons regarding their creativity), "Giving expression to
your soul has no price—it is invaluable. Play your music. Play with your
focus only on the music. Let the music and the song of your soul guide
your life. Follow the flow from the inside rather than setting up limitations from the outside. Live into your beauty." Though I am speaking
as a parent, I speak this way with authority because I know the potential
of our inherently creative energy for my clients, for myself, and for you.

Creative expression and feeling creative are inextricably correlated
with the vitality, wholeness, energetic vibrance, and personal satisfaction I have witnessed among clients in my healing practice. Creative
currency is the wealth of the future, and each one of us is entitled to
its flow. When we create in this way, from the natural movement of
spirit coming through us, the creative process has an inherently spiritual component. And we bring this spirit potential into a particular
form—a new relationship, a way of working, a piece of art, an aspect
of healing, a solution to a problem, a business, or a new life direction.
Working with the creative current in the center of your life is not just
being creative but is an opportunity to live "inspired" or "with spirit."

Some of the many definitions of spirit are these: *breath, courage, vigor, soul,* or *life*. Outside of any particular religious framework, my personal experience of connecting with the creative life force is that it brings a direct connection with spirit and its multitude of forms. Tapping into the creative energy expands us and brings an essence—a vibration—that contains the sacred and mysterious qualities of spirit to whatever is being made.

Attune with Creative Rhythms

Creative currents flow around us constantly. Each day and every creative cycle has a rhythm within that we can attune ourselves to and synchronize with. We know these rhythms in our bodies but may have forgotten how to feel them or sense the aliveness that occurs in the presence of spirit. For many, it is like a lost language; it takes work to remember how to speak it and to quiet the critical voice that is so embodied in the rational culture that denies its presence.

If you want to deepen your daily relationship with the creative expression of spirit to know what "spirit" is for you, begin to look for these rhythms in various aspects of your life. True creative abundance requires attuning one's own energy field and then aligning with the greater creative rhythms contained in a creative cycle. I identify five components or rhythms of a creative cycle: *invitation, preparation, inspiration, celebration,* and *restoration*.

By becoming aware of the qualities of different creative phases, you have greater ability to read where you might be in a cycle. In this way, you can align with the movement instead of trying to access a different part of the cycle, or you can focus on the qualities of a particular rhythm in order to support the cycle's completion. For example, getting too focused on the exciting first phase of invitation means you will be continuously inspired but may not have many complete creations to show for it, because you are not taking any one creation through a full creative cycle. Like jumping from job to job or project to project, moving on before completing a full developmental cycle means you will only engage the superficial aspects of the creative process rather than the more layered ones that arise with repetition and time.

Knowing how to identify the various qualities of a creative movement in our lives allows us to be creative while also attending to the details of living. Just as a farmer knows the right time to plant, fertilize, irrigate, or harvest, if you are in tune with your rhythmic flows, you will better know how to cultivate your various creations and their particular stages of development.

While the movement of spirit may follow a cycle in the process of being creative, this is not a rigid structure. Tending to spirit is living under the open sky. You are untethered and this is your greatest joy; you are untethered and this is your greatest fear. May these rhythms assist your creativity as you give rise to form.

Invitation

Invitation is the first creative impulse: the invitation to be creative. An invitation may arise as a new work opportunity, a relationship change, a pregnancy, a healing crisis, or even a reflection of who we are becoming. If we follow the workings of spirit, we see how spirit invites us to the places that expand our creative potential. Each invitation is the first glimpse of what is unfolding but has yet to fully manifest.

An invitation from spirit carries a sense of something new. Feelings may arise, from excitement to fear—a range of emotions that reflect the way you have learned to greet the unknown. Notice how you tend to respond to a new potential and discover a signal for paying close attention to what is arising in order to accept this creative invitation from spirit.

Exercise: Receiving an Invitation

With a pad of paper and pen close by, find a quiet place, bringing your breath and awareness to your center.

- *Reflections*: Think about what you are making in your life. How is spirit inviting you to create? What does the energy of this invitation feel like? Be aware of any sensations, images, or feelings that arise. Notice the invitation from spirit and how it touches your body and being. Feel where you are easily touched and where you would like to make room for spirit.

- *Creative Action*: Take a piece of paper and write down everything that you are creating or are desiring to create in your life; list whatever comes to mind. When you are finished, look at the list and focus on two essential invitations. Write down the invitations on a separate piece of paper and place them where they can remind you of how spirit is calling.

Preparation

Preparation is the first movement of integrating an invitation. It is clearing space and gathering tools so that when the creative energy comes, you can move into a new potential. It is cleaning out the garden shed or organizing your paint and canvases. It is saying yes to an invitation and building the structure to hold your creative essence.

Preparation means doing the work and searching for the knowledge that frees our understanding. We clean house. We wash clothes. All the while, we may keep company with spirit if we remain conscious of breath and the quality of our presence. It is possible to become lost in the movement of preparation by doing task upon task or procrastinating. To know the difference, feel into your center to identify your creative priorities before you begin. Sometimes putting something off is also allowing the energy to line up. Either way, mindful preparation is guided by the invitation received. Preparation may involve the task aspects of working on a particular creative project, but it can also involve clearing the creative space or even doing self-care or personal healing that, while not directly related to the project, will influence the wholeness of the overall energy infusing the creation.

The preparation movement is typically more task oriented, but it still follows the creative flow from the original invitation, eventually bringing us to our inspiration. The path we take, even appearing as a detour to growth or new ground at times, is a part of this preparation. What are we preparing for? We may not even know until the moment when it—spirit—arrives.

Exercise: Preparing for Spirit

With a pad of paper and pen close by, find a quiet place, bringing your breath and awareness to your center.

- *Reflections*: Think about the recent activities in your life. How are these actions preparing your next form of expression? Are there habits or activities that are distracting you from your relationship with spirit or creative essence? What additional spirit-focused preparation is necessary to support your creative expression or expansion?
- *Creative Action*: Take a piece of paper and complete the following statement: "I am preparing to engage my creative essence by . . ." and then list whatever comes to mind. Write for as long as is needed. When you are finished, look at this list and select three actions to take as preparation for this creative invitation.

Your preparation may be physical (like doing yoga or cleaning the house), mental (making time for your creative life and changing self-limiting concepts), emotional (processing old feelings and asking for the help that you need), or structural (reorganizing the office, making a creative space, or procuring child care). Each act of preparation clears your energy and readies you to receive further inspiration, enabling the next creative movement. Mindful preparation can be a sacred act, with the intention of clearing a path to spirit. Preparation can also be the discomfort of moving toward your dreams. It can be easier to strive for a dream than to commit to the risks and rewards of manifesting a dream. Be prepared to address your own resistance in order to transition into the next creative rhythm.

Inspiration

Inspiration is literally "something inspired," or the receipt of spirit. It is a divine influence directly exerted on the soul. This influence is both liberating and disorienting because it takes us wherever it will. And if we allow ourselves to be moved, we will more fully receive our inspiration. Too often, however, people become afraid and try to control something that is inherently wild and fleeting.

Inspiration is not the excitement of the initial call; it is feeling our divine essence within us responding to the creative movement we have prepared for. Spirit comes close, and we feel its wildness. Spirit comes closer, and we feel our own wildness respond. All of life responds to its energy. This is why our tolerance for chaos must increase in order for us to be in close proximity to spirit—particularly when you are working at your creative edge and allowing creative energy to expand your potential. Just like labor and birth, the intensity of the expansion is felt in your center. Prior to the creative movement of inspiration, the energy around you quickens, and you may notice that your body feels compressed. These are the signals that announce the potential for encountering spirit.

Let go of the urge to flee when intensity and a sense of inner chaos build; the form within is being pressed and changed. Stay with the discomfort as long as you can. The physical, emotional, and/or spiritual compression you feel is your resistance to your expansion. Surrender the tension in your body, the resistance in your mind, and the hesitation in your heart. Surrender, and you will fill with new life.

The intensity of natural chaos is inherent in the world of nature, but how that plays out in our increasingly organized lives can seem like an abstract concept. Nassim Nicholas Taleb, a professor of risk engineering at the Polytechnic Institute of New York University, studies the effects of natural chaos and the benefits that can arise from disorder and the change of order. In his *Wall Street Journal* article entitled "Learning to Love Volatility," Taleb suggests that we learn to be less fragile and tolerate some level of volatility. "Natural or organic systems are anti-fragile: They need some dose of disorder in order to develop. Deprive your bones of stress and they become brittle," says Taleb. Though the focus in modern times has been comfort and stability, Taleb states that "by making ourselves too comfortable and eliminating all volatility from our lives, we . . . [make] our bodies and souls . . . fragile."[18] And we lose touch with the potential that comes from remaining in contact with natural creative forces that are required to forge new patterns and ways of being.

Though order is typically a high value for most people, Taleb also relays his view that in economic life and history, just about everything of consequence arises from "black swans," what Taleb calls: "large events that are both unexpected and highly consequential . . . 9/11, the internet, the rise of Google."[19] He reminds us that some stress can be helpful for health, and that our bodies need variety in terrain; and that people mention posttraumatic stress disorder, but there are no accounts of posttraumatic growth. Likewise, the tendency to control chaos, as with fire suppression, tends to create more volatility (extreme heat, out-of-control fires) than does learning how to work with the pattern of disorder that arises naturally.

Naturally occurring chaos is not to be confused with busyness or self-imposed stress. Disorder that happens in the midst of tending spirit has the quality of a storm. One day, I was walking with my boys when the rain caught us out in the open. The drops fell lightly at first, but the air prickled with energy. We gathered beneath a playground slide just as the rain began to splash down. I wrapped my shawl around my head and shoulders, holding my arms like wings around my sons.

We sat with our faces almost touching, my hat poking up out of our makeshift tent. The water fell and bounced until tiny rivers formed at our feet. We were giddy, huddled together, feeling the wildness surround us. Typically, we experience a storm only by looking out the window, but my boys and I felt the intensity of this storm differently because we were outside in the midst of it. Its taste was in our mouths, our skin separated from its wet embrace by only a thin layer of wool. Being in the storm, I was struck by the feeling of building pressure that occurred as the storm moved in, just as it does with all naturally occurring chaos. Rather than a constant pressure, this type of volatility builds and intensifies, then releases—just like a birth, a storm, or the natural disorder Taleb describes.

The entire movement of inspiration is brief but intense. We are energized when, rather than resisting it, we give in to its rhythm: a crescendo of activity whose pounding pulse steadily increases. It pounds like a drum, asking us to respond—to be moved. Then the beat slows, gradually returning to calm. In contrast, stress is more constant and oppressive. By recognizing the difference, we can look for the still point in the midst of our chaos. From there, we experience the awesome nature of spirit and the sense of aliveness that arises from creating and being inspired, so that we ourselves are changed in the process.

Exercise: Receiving Inspiration

With a pad of paper and pen close by, find a quiet place, bringing your breath and awareness to your center.

- *Reflections*: Think about how you are inspired in your life. Where is your greatest burst of expression happening? What form is your inspiration taking? Where are you allowing the type of disorder or risk that assists creative inspiration and expansion?
- *Creative Action*: Take a piece of paper and complete the statement: "I am inspired or moved by spirit when I . . ." and then list whatever comes to mind. Write for as long as you need. When you are finished,

choose an action from your list and direct more energy toward receiving this inspiration.

Receiving the inspiration of spirit involves freeing your expression in words, thoughts, feelings, movements, and ways of being. It means allowing yourself to get bigger, more joyful, sillier, sadder, crazier, and messier. Inspiration requires letting go of all resistance so spirit can pour through your being: *you are filled with breath, courage, vigor, soul, life.*

Celebration

Celebration is the point of breakthrough—the summit of the mountain, the moment of birth, the ultimate realization. It is the opening that comes after surmounting many obstacles, the peace that arrives after a storm. Celebration is our union with spirit. We long for this movement that allows us to see the truth of our lives. And we do encounter what we have been searching for, though not always in the manner we expect. It happens most often when we are not looking but are fully immersed in our creative process.

Celebration is the moment when spirit gives us our truth, but it comes when it will. If we are paying attention, we recognize what has been revealed.

Exercise: Making Celebration

With a pad of paper and pen close by, find a quiet place, bringing your breath and awareness to your center.

- *Reflections*: Reflect on the recent movements of spirit in your life. Think about victories and breakthroughs in your personal evolution. What do you have to celebrate? How are you celebrating these pinnacles on your path?
- *Creative Action*: Take a piece of paper and complete the following statement: "I want to celebrate my work with spirit in . . ." and write

until it feels complete. When you have finished, take this statement as a commitment to celebrate your work with spirit. Look for tangible ways to actively celebrate and acknowledge your progress on the journey thus far, like gathering with friends or taking yourself out.

As you near a time of celebration or creative breakthrough, notice the transformation that signals your rebirth; you must be able to stand the pressure that builds just before you emerge into new life. If you are in a particularly difficult place of expansion, know that you are stretching toward an even greater, more joyous celebration. Celebration is your truth, but to reach it, you must face your toughest restrictions. And when you arrive, you will celebrate your own regeneration.

Restoration

Restoration is the end and also the beginning of each creative cycle. In this movement, we integrate the sustenance of our soul into daily being; we turn the wisdom of engaging our creative essence into the actions of our everyday lives; we take inspiration and find our form, knowing all along that we are also preparing ourselves for the next invitation from spirit.

Restoration is the homecoming; you return from your journey to process all that you have seen. You are renewed with each full cycle, especially when you take the time to process what has been received. Allowing a full integration before moving into another creative cycle provides satisfaction and a sense of completion. Some cycles find their completion in a day, while others continue for several months or years. Stop and rest, taking notice of where you are. Then start keeping company with spirit again.

Exercise: Finding Restoration

With a pad of paper and pen close by, find a quiet place, bringing your breath and awareness to your center.

- *Reflections*: Reflect on your recent creative cycles and movements with spirit. How has your creative essence evolved? How is your creativity finding form or being integrated into your daily life? How are you restoring the energy used in this creative cycle?
- *Creative Action*: Take a piece of paper and complete the following statement: "I am integrating this creative movement by . . ." and write until it feels complete. When you are finished, select three ways to begin your restoration.

Restoration is returning from your creative cycle to put everything in its place. It is a time of replenishment after the creative outpouring and the release of what is no longer needed. It is the movement that strengthens what you have learned as you rest, eat, and ponder your experiences.

By traveling through these five rhythms, you have experienced a complete creative cycle: receiving an *invitation*; doing the *preparation* that allows you to step into the creative current; following the direction long enough that you find *inspiration*, filled with the presence of spirit; reaching the *celebration* point of truth, knowledge, expansion, or breakthrough that arises from this creative connection; and taking time for *restoration*, processing and integrating what you received.

The next time you receive a creative invitation, be intentional about whether to say yes; and then be sure to travel fully through each rhythm. In doing so, you will notice that the creative cycle is boldly expansive and deeply nourishing for your wild creative soul.

Deconstruct the Box and Make New Forms

In contrast to actively creating our lives from the center of our heart-felt desires or movements of spirit, we have likely crafted these forms around the business of building a livelihood. Again, by following the linear models that were established by years of schooling, many of our lives are initially shaped by degree requirements and school schedules. Beyond school, our days may be organized around an eight-to-five, Monday-through-Friday work schedule. Inadvertently, the skill that's most developed is the formation of a personal life around these defined edges, rather than the engagement or interaction with these forms in a more direct manner.

From work schedules and professions to roles, identities, and relationships, we can take apart and rebuild the boxes or lines that define the shape of our lives to form structures that actually serve us. We can smooth, strip away, or redefine the layers we carry in our physical forms and energetic flow so we can more readily express our true essence. In fact, if we are in touch with our creative flow, we will be cultivating forms to fit the life we desire rather than shaping our lives in the manner dictated by a particular external form.

Dynamic Forms: A Place to Be Creative

Since the routines of work and living dictate how we use our energy, we must create dynamic forms that give us a place to be creative. The forms that define our daily rhythms—whether as professions, habits, exercise routines, partnerships, or ways of being—can be supportive structures that hold our energy or rigid ones that are tired and uninspired. Examine the structures in your life and determine whether they add to or diminish your creativity.

Moving beyond a regular form by taking a new route to work, eating at a new restaurant, or trying a new style can shake up your routine and bring insight or inspiration. Traveling transports you outside of your regular forms in the same way, bringing shifts on all levels. Even staying at home but putting yourself in the frame of mind of a traveler—seeing your neighborhood and your environs anew—can be revitalizing. Though you might crave (and indeed need) routine, also invite the opportunity for new ways of being. Try living in the more fluid place of open time, where creative impulses reign, and invite those around you to join in.

Reflect on the layers of identity that define you and how you might want to change these defining lines to better reflect who you want to be. For example, if you developed your sense of self through achievement and striving, you may have lost touch with your own desires. Or if you didn't know the value of your creative essence, you may have stopped engaging with it. Coming back into relationship with the creative channel of your life flow will often reform the layers that give expression to your identity. Even the expectations you establish for yourself in the various aspects of your life can become limiting or rigid. As you become creative in how you see and express yourself, as well as in your expectations for personal or creative success, the forms you inhabit become more dynamic and able to change as needed. Creating dynamic forms leaves new room for spiritual assistance and new ways of being, beyond your imagination.

Energy Session: Moving Beyond the Provider Role

When I began to offer energy sessions for male partners and friends of my clients, I found that men needed just as much support to restore creative-energy flow and authentic creativity as women. Adam came for a session to revive a sense of passion in his life. He had last felt truly inspired more than fifteen years earlier, as a young man heading off to travel in Europe. He had experienced glimpses of his passions over the years but nothing that was sustained as he developed a career and became a father to two children.

As we began, I suggested that he seemed to be carrying a great weight. Delving into his energy burden, he expressed feeling financially responsible to provide for his family and, as a result, trapped in his current work. He had also experienced a sense of loss when an early company he launched failed; and recently, an uncle who had been a key mentor had died. I asked if he had fully processed the grief of both losses—which, though distinctly different, could weigh on his energy.

Adam said that he had not explored his feelings, coming as he did from a long line of stoic males. I suggested that he do so in a creative manner: rather than counseling or working with the story of his grief, he could take an art class (for example), and address the laden feeling in his center—the held grief, the feeling of being overly responsible, the sense of being stuck, and much more. Adam needed to perceive difficult feelings not as signs of weakness or lack of capability but as source material for powerful creations.

Adam wanted to take a metal-working class. Though it was not directly related to the present challenges in his energy field or his life, I suggested that being creative in a hands-on manner might move stagnant energies, increase creativity, and bring fresh inspiration. Having a place where he felt free to be creative could be liberating and even inspire new identities beyond serving as the family provider. Setting down the burdens of past grief and financial stress by working with creative energy in a freer form could help Adam feel free within himself.

As Adam imagined the hands-on feeling of taking the metal-working class, his whole energy field brightened. He left the session intending to engage his creative energy to move the denser energies out of his field and turn his attention toward new possibilities.

Redefining Your Roles

In restoring the feminine and redefining the masculine, we all need to heal the divisions caused by rigid gender roles that diminish our unique expression and ways of relating with one another. Both men and women have been hampered by the restrictive lines that define gender, relationship, sexuality, femininity, and masculinity, and all the expectations built upon these definitions. Women have been exploring their roles and redefining them through the feminist movement, but the next feminist wave needs to recover the feminine and feminine modes of being, rather than simply joining the unbalanced masculine models that men have followed for decades.

Men are realizing that being defined as the income earner and measuring success by the ability to provide are as burdensome as being restricted to the home was for many women. The focus on having a career has kept many men from developing or even knowing their inner realms, leaving them profoundly unsatisfied. At the same time, they often experience shame, whether inflicted by themselves or others, when they are not following traditional paths or when they find success elusive. I am heartened to witness increasing numbers of men working to change this, and I work to assist men in reclaiming their rightful full expression of self. One of these efforts is The Good Men Project (goodmenproject.com), a platform to explore modern manhood and the question "What does it mean to be a good man?" The mind-expanding articles and information on this site offer a valuable lens through which to see the challenges men face in regard to gender limitations, ideas for them to take more responsibility for their personal transformation, and ways both genders might access new ways of being.

In the process of raising boys, I have come into contact with the entrenched male code that exists in many aspects of culture and within all of us. It's beyond time to have platforms and discussions about male gender roles and how to redefine them. Men have just as much depth as women; they only have less cultural permission to explore and express it. They have a radiance that is rarely acknowledged or fully expressed when they lose touch with the creative center. In this time, as men and women redefine success to include their own wholeness, we can work together to create lives built from and reflective of the capacity we wish to embody.

Exercise: Redefining Your Roles

Take a moment to ponder the roles you inhabit and how they give definition to your life. How you would like to change them to better express your full radiance? Find a pad, a pen, and a quiet place to work.

1. List the primary roles you inhabit—partner, wife/husband, mother/father, consultant, daughter/son, businessperson, homemaker, gardener—drawing a circle around each one with enough room to write more.
2. List all of the traits that come to mind with each role, whether positive or negative. List them freely within each circle containing each role.
3. List any roles you would like to have in your life, putting each one in another circle (such as artist, healer, writer, dancer, lover, or teacher).
4. Again, list all of the traits associated with these roles.
5. Reflect on your outline. Where do the roles seem limited by gender or otherwise restricted? How are they in need of more room for expression or redefinition? Where do they feel naturally expansive? How would you like to bring in a new form or role? How would taking on a new role or redefining these lines change your creativity or your relationship with others? Use your creative thinking to redefine these lines in ways that expand rather than restrict who you are.
6. Place stars beside the top three roles you would like to focus on, or even make up new words to redefine who you are becoming. Remember that you can continually redefine these roles as your creativity evolves and reveals new modes of being in your energy field and daily life.

The Potential in Creativity

Creativity has the potential to transform the limiting patterns found in any role or job or the linear models that drive us into depletion and exhaustion. Once, when I was having a routine checkup at my neighborhood healthcare clinic, I crossed paths with a young nurse practitioner who was ordinarily passionate but seemed weary that day. I inquired about how she was doing. She answered that, in regard to her work, she was just trying to keep her head above water. We talked about the brokenness of the mainstream medical system; with the number of clients a provider like her sees in a day, there is no time for the depth of care the provider and the patient desire. Today's medical providers often feel like they are just managing crises and doling out medication while exhausting themselves. I asked, "What do you really want to do?" She answered, "I want to work in women's health with clients who are more holistically oriented so I can address health issues preventatively—but I don't know where to begin."

I told her about my experience of leaving the hospital setting as a physical therapist: while my job at the hospital provided security, it also limited my time and the way I could practice care. She sighed, "Maybe I'll get to it someday." I encouraged her to begin now, at least by setting intentions and thinking about the way she wanted to practice care and structure her work life. It is always possible to make a change with creative thinking, but we have to be willing to engage this capacity rather than live in the status quo.

Creativity can assist us in so many ways, including our response to a difficult challenge. When a male client shared his frustrations with an intimate relationship, I encouraged him to be creative about it—to look from new perspectives or try new approaches to address the challenges with his partner. When another client spoke about her decision to apply to graduate school because she was frustrated in her job and did not know how to make a transition, I suggested that leaving a situation and moving into another without shifting the core energy pattern often results in the creation of a new problem. When she looked more closely at the situation, she realized that her schedule and sense of value were what she wanted to redefine. With this knowledge, she saw that perhaps it could happen in the context of her job if she asked for what she wanted. Creative potential engages the part of ourselves that can find solutions; and we know we are using this potential when we identify many different types of solutions rather than either/or options.

Most people have aspects of creative potential that they draw upon or even use on a daily basis, but may not label as creative. For example, my rancher mother-in-law does not perceive herself as creative, yet her creativity with food enables her to make a delightful meal out of the simplest farm-sourced ingredients. Likewise, she turned a small farm into a home for an award-winning flock of prized Suffolk ewes. She has also used her creative abilities in 4-H activities, working with young people in a way that enabled her own children to gain the skills of leadership, project management, and negotiation—skills that would prepare them to use creativity in applied ways.

Creativity is a resource for savoring life as well as a handy tool in times of stress. When we encounter any kind of difficulty, our energy field tends to constrict in response. By breathing into the full spaciousness around us, becoming aware of the vast potential in our energy field and the universe it connects us to, we can change the way we respond and even the resources we draw from. Regardless of outer circumstances, we can align the energy center to enhance our energy resources. I teach this simple technique of aligning and cultivating resonance or harmony in the energy field to clients who are going through divorce, working through times of monetary strain, dealing with challenging family members, experiencing a health crisis, or navigating any time that the flow of life is moving counter to what they might desire (see the exercise "Creating a Resonant Energy Field" on page 198). The events of life may ebb and flow, but we can always inhabit our full creative potential to receive the vast support it contains for us.

Even someone who identifies as creative may need to remember the personal applications of creativity. A designer I worked with was clearly creative in many aspects of her life—her profession, her dress, her ability to create for others—but sometimes she forgot her own self in the process. She became so caught up in generating creative designs for others that she lost track of what she wanted to create for herself. Creativity is a resource, but like any resource, it is better used in a sustainable and intentional manner. The creative channel is related to your life flow and your life purpose; it's a resource to treasure and use wisely.

Embrace Your Creative Journey

Seth Godin writes, "Art isn't a result; it's a journey. The challenge of our time is to find a journey worthy of your heart and soul."[20] This is apt advice for setting down the linear pathways that overemphasize results and finding instead the more holistic models of living—models that value the journey. However, it's not just any journey we might seek; as Godin suggests, it's one that is "worthy of your heart and soul." What journey would you take that is worthy of your heart and soul? Is your life entwined with this journey so far? I would also add that, in addition to seeking a heart and soul–based direction, the challenge is to build a framework to sustain you along the way. Since many of our present-day structures are not based on journeys of the heart and soul, you often have to rebuild your framework in order to make such a quest, learning how to read the creative signs that offer guidance when the trail becomes faint.

Finding Your Way: Reading the Creative Signs

Sometimes when you are in the middle of a project, it's difficult to know whether a particular challenge means you need to try another direction or drop the project altogether. But in reading the energy signs, you will find an inner measure of how the project is going, even when the outer signs are unclear. These inner signs contain valuable directions when you know how to read them.

One way to follow the underlying creative signs is to look for the pattern of flow. Notice where the flow is in regard to a creative project, and direct your energy there. If a particular direction is blocked, move in the direction of flow rather than pushing against the block. Following the flow may lead you in a new or alternate direction that will better support the overall creative process.

Patterns of flow align with patterns of synchronicity; so, where you encounter synchronicity, you will find flow. Synchronicity is an oft-used term (originally coined by Swiss psychologist Carl Jung), defined as two or more unrelated events that may be meaningful or relay an underlying pattern. Jung suggested that concurrent events can be related to a larger underlying framework, such as the collective unconscious, which could also be a description of the greater creative-energy field. For example, after I self-published my first book, I felt an intuition that it would still benefit from an official publisher to hold it in the long term. Rather than contacting publishers directly, I began talking to people in my community when the topic of the book came up naturally. During one of those conversations, a friend suggested Beyond Words as a publisher and mentioned a personal contact with one of the founders of the company. I listened to the suggestion but reflected on it instead of taking immediate action (receiving the feminine guidance before acting with the masculine). A few days later, I opened the local newspaper to find that the same Beyond Words cofounder my friend had mentioned was featured on a panel at the Wordstock literary festival in Portland. I recognized the synchronicity between my desire to find a publisher, my friend's advice, and an opportunity to meet the same person my friend had suggested. I made plans to attend the event, though I had only a brief window in my schedule.

I arrived at Wordstock just as the panel was finishing. I had missed the introductions of the panelists but walked up to the person nearest to me. She pointed to the person I sought, who was already making her way to the door. I strode up to her and introduced myself, asking if I could give her a copy of my self-published *Wild Feminine*. It's a risk to extend oneself at an event like this with no personal introduction, but I did so because of the pattern of synchronicity. I didn't give her a hard sell regarding the books because I trusted the overall flow I had learned to move with. Later, when we were friends, she told me that if I had approached her even six months earlier, they would likely have rejected the project. But my timing was ideal; this spiritually oriented publisher was just now moving into the realm of the body. Beyond Words ultimately published three of my books as a result of my following the creative flow to the natural timing of our connection. Observing patterns of flow and synchronistic events in one's life provides guidance for reading the creative signs and directing creative energy.

When a barrier is truly present, that suggests an alternate direction or the end of a creative cycle; there is a halted energy flow in one's center with no real alternate flow. If the creative-energy current has stopped and you are still trying to push the creative process forward, it may be that you are attached to a certain outcome; or you are trying to hold on in order to assert your will or reaffirm your value. While it's natural to want to be valued for what you can make or do, it's more sustainable to know your value as an inherent truth rather than link it to a particular creation. Trying to make a creative project come to life (or receive recognition) in order to affirm your value is generally a recipe for more struggle, especially when there is no energy flow to sustain it. Also, the timing of the project may be off; but when it doesn't come to fruition, you feel less valuable personally, having linked it with your value. Our value is meant to be intact regardless of what we create, and our creations are a way of sharing our intrinsic worth.

When a creation or a creative dream is not finding its form, there are usually external forces at play. Instead of forging ahead in a masculine manner, try a feminine approach: Be still and listen. Seek insight from those around you. Bring awareness to the left, more feminine hemisphere of your energy field. Notice whether your feminine field is open to receive. Think about where creative energy is flowing and the abundance you already have. Ask for signs and guidance from the divine. Receive the insight that comes.

A creation can be ahead of its time; and it may not be recognized, at least initially, because of this. Creative visionaries are, by definition, ahead of their audience. Therefore, the audience may not yet have the framework to be able to receive a visionary creation. If multiple publishers turn down a project, for example, they may not be able to see the brilliance of the creation; but this may also mean that readers will not be able to see it either. How many artists have struggled in their lifetime only to be celebrated posthumously?

This is the point to clarify: when you encounter blocks to bringing your creative work into being, are you contining to follow this particular creative path based on the guidance and inspiration in your center or as a means of validation or some other outcome you hope to receive? Answering this question will clarify how to proceed. Searching outside your center for a sense of creative meaning, you rarely receive the inner sustenance you need on a soul level. If, however, your creative process is guided by an expression of your spirit and a sense of internal flow, persevere until your creation finds the light of day; it will heal and redefine your creative range along the way.

Where are you in the flow of your overall creative cycle?
Have you ever willed a creation to happen? What did you learn?
Are there any creative projects you'd now like to take through a whole cycle?

The Creative Journey as a Transformative Process

The whole point of engaging your creative essence as a practice of keeping company with spirit is to more fully express the unique imprint of your soul. Spirit energy moves through you and into your life as a person, partner, lover, child, parent, professional, neighbor, and creative being. There is nothing more satisfying than living each day with the full light of your expression meeting the world. However, a common myth about realizing your dreams is that it will be a solely joyful experience. While having a dream come true can bring joy, it can also reveal the resistance and restrictive patterns within your energy field that limit joy or creative potential.

Many of us are wired for scarcity and the struggle that we perceive as being required to achieve our dreams. When you realize a dream, you may express such pent-up feelings as fear, anger, or grief. Or you may encounter a shadow aspect of yourself—a part of you that does not feel comfortable with realized dreams and creative radiance. In realizing your dream, you may need to move past the resistance of your imprinted creative field or perhaps redefine your creative identity. It may require work to recover your expression, to find the words that have gone unsaid, to rediscover latent parts of yourself. To keep expanding your creative range and manifesting your dreams means you need to work with feelings and shadow aspects of the self that arise in the process, particularly when you are changing your imprinted family code by doing so. Rather than ignoring these aspects or feeling ashamed when they threaten to block your progress, explore them with curiosity to learn what they are telling you about your untapped potential. In this way, the creative journey continues to be a profoundly transformative process.

Exercise: Transforming Your Creative Self

In the midst of your creative process, you may find yourself transformed as well. Reflect on the following questions for insight and support.

- *Invitation*: What new aspect of my expression am I being invited to engage?
- *Preparation*: What action will enable me to follow this new direction? What deeper need is calling for my attention, or how can I support myself in the overall process?
- *Inspiration*: What feeling or sensation arises just before and during this particular creative movement? What can I sense in my body? How can I allow spirit to assist me?

- *Celebration*: When I follow this new direction, what greater potential do I access? Where is my creative range expanding?
- *Restoration*: How can I integrate this new potential into my living practices?

How to Meet Your Shadow

Your shadow is a place in your energy field that you may avoid because it relates to what you would rather not see about yourself. By meeting your shadow with curiosity, you have the opportunity to look at those things that interfere with living your full potential. Keeping watch for your shadow, you gain an ally that shows you where to do your work. For example, going against the creative flow because you are attached to a particular direction as a form of achievement, even when the flow is suggesting another direction, shows you where to work on your sense of inner value and your faith in creative cycles. Or investing in a full creative cycle but then shying away from the recognition this new potential invites reveals your discomfort with being acknowledged or seen in a new way. When you recognize those aspects of yourself that have previously existed only in shadow, they will no longer wield their unconscious influence in your life. By bringing each part of your being into the light, you discover the tools that will assist your creative and spiritual development. Meeting your shadow allows you to see more clearly.

Embracing the Spiral Pathway

Realigning with spirit is a spiral pathway rather than a linear progression. Each situation you encounter is simply another turn in your spiritual journey; and you will witness similar themes in your life over and over again. This does not depict failure but is simply a part of the spiral path.

When an experience is familiar and also challenges you, pay attention to its layers of expression. By looking closely, you will see that what faces you is not the same as before. You have traveled far enough along the spiral and worked through your limitations enough that your capacities for being creative and keeping company with spirit have expanded. The similarity of what lies before you is the signal that you have made another turn in your journey. This occasion will both validate what you have learned thus far and offer new opportunities for growth. The continued growth of your soul requires that challenges increase along with your expanding skills as you travel this path.

Putting Concepts into Practice

In my life, I carry the energy of the pioneer in my lineage as both a foundation of my personality and a way of working with creative energy. Many of my ancestors migrated to the American West as pioneers; and from this part of myself, I have found a tremendous capacity to forge new trails. At the same time, I often find myself drawn in multiple directions.

When I am working through the shadow of the pioneer archetype, there is a temptation to leave behind whatever I have built each time I am newly inspired. Being conscious of the shadow aspect of the pioneer in myself, I find creative inspiration in this energy but then choose to develop only two or three paths. I return my focus to my creations until I find a place for them. I may integrate previous creations into my present movement, set them aside for a period, or release them if they no longer serve a vital purpose.

Traveling the spiral pathway means I will meet myself as pioneer over and over again. The more I call the pioneer into my life, the more I appreciate this lineage aspect that enables my forging of new ground. Yet I also remind her of the value of rest and home.

Rebuilding Your Foundation

As you live a creative life with intention, you will find structures in your life that support the presence of spirit as well as those that inhibit this connection. Reinforce the structures that are beneficial and rebuild those in need of change; in this process, you will likely be disoriented at times. Just keep asking yourself what you need, and then create the structures to serve you.

There are different ways to rebuild your foundation: sometimes starting over is the only way to make what you want; at other times, you can build a bridge between two places until you are ready to cross over. For example, changing inner dialogue from self-defeating to encouraging requires switching your words whenever you notice your old pattern. The new words you choose become the bridge for taking you into a new way of being with yourself. Eventually, the bridge becomes unnecessary because you begin to rely more often on the structure of the beneficial words that offer support for your well-being.

Rebuilding your foundation allows you to change your creative energy. This can include addressing different aspects that affect creative flow, such as the alignment of your body, the feng shui of your home, the way you live, the practice of your creativity, your relationships, your schedule, or your daily focus. In order to enhance the creative flow moving from within your center into all aspects of your life, it is worth rebuilding foundations to offer yourself the best support.

Bringing Spirit into Form through Ritual

Another aspect of working with creative rhythms to bring spirit into tangible form is to use these rhythms to make rituals. Rituals offer a way to connect with spirit, and they give expression to those otherwise inaccessible energies and held emotions that limit your creative range.

Unacknowledged feelings tend to be held in the body, and carrying these dormant feelings is an energetic and physical burden. Even walling off a particular feeling requires holding tension in the body. This tension then interferes with the core ease and energy movement in the body, diminishing the capacity for creative expression.

Grief is a commonly held emotion in the human body, often passed along—rather than expressed—within families. This is particularly true because of the general absence of grief rituals in Western culture. In an effort to address my held grief and transform the range of expression that I pass along to my children, I created a grief ritual for my family. Although the acts of this ritual are simple, the presence of spirit we feel in this process is quite profound. I invite you to use this ritual exercise or to create one of your own, releasing stored energy to make more room for your creative abundance.

Exercise: Revisiting the Creation—A Grief Ritual

- *Invitation*: Gather with a group of friends and/or family. Invite them to inwardly reflect on the grief they carry, both as individuals and as a part of their lineage.
- *Preparation*: Distribute paper, pens, and string. Each person writes words that express their grief on individual pieces of paper. Each paper will then be tied together onto a stick that will either be burned or thrown into a river, whichever you choose.
- *Inspiration*: Begin to write, allowing each person to write their words of grief for as long as needed. Those who have finished can fold and tie their paper onto the stick.
- *Celebration*: Choose someone to throw the stick into the fire or the water. In the meantime, everyone else claps, chants, cheers, watches, or does what they are moved to do.
- *Restoration*: Come back to the circle and share observations with one another. On one piece of paper, write words of hope or prayers that can be taken home and placed on an altar or in a garden space. If time permits, have a meal together, and notice any changes in your energy and the energy of your community.

Working with retained feelings through ritual or other ways of enhancing expression will encourage the movement of your creative energy and enliven your creations. Simple rituals can also energize your intentions. During one busy creative period, I did not have time for a ritualized gathering of women, yet I wanted to be intentional about what I was deliberately releasing in order to embrace my desired focus. So, a friend and I set up a simple new-moon intention series over a period of nine months. Though she lived in Hawaii and I lived in Oregon, we set up our ritual through email.

We chose the new moon for our ritual because it is a natural time of release (this is the time when women's bodies tend to release their menstrual blood in the absence of artificial light or other disruptions). Near the new moon, we respectively emailed our intentions for release and what we desired to receive in place of the release. Then, on the new moon, each one of us did our own simple ritual with both sets of intentions as a way of holding and energizing our creative dreams together. Sometimes I made a fire and burned what we had written to release the intentions to spirit. At other times, I buried the intentions in my yard or at the base of an ancient tree near my home; or I whispered them into the wind with a prayer. My friend did the same. This ritual process was simple and doable, but what gives power to a ritual is having a clear intention and then opening to the movements of spirit. I was thankful for this sisterhood that carried me through one creative season and the energy that arose with our ritualized intention.

Tending Your Creations with Spirit

Another way to enhance your connection with spirit and the quality of energy you create in everyday life is to look for the essence of spirit wherever you are, reclaiming the sacred in the midst of living.

A friend of mine who is a nun once told me about her experience at a personal retreat. Each participant was assigned multiple duties to care for the property and retreat center; and she found herself resenting these tasks, longing for more time in quiet meditation. Then, in the midst of hanging laundry, she understood a simple truth: the sense of aliveness she experienced in prayerful meditation could be with her regardless of what she was doing. Being with spirit did not depend on her activity but on her willingness to accept spirit in every moment.

Every day you can choose whether or not to overcome your places of resistance and attend to the details of life with spirit. On creative journeys (like all spiritual and life journeys), you may encounter challenges as a part of your personal growth. But the creations you tend assist you in meeting your shadow and engaging the obstacles that will ultimately free your expression.

Exercise: Tending Your Creations with Spirit
Find a quiet place to reflect on the following questions.

- *Invitation*: What is my creation or creative process inviting me to do at this moment?
- *Preparation*: What creative practice will allow me to freely receive this invitation?
- *Inspiration*: When I look deeply into this moment, what do I feel like doing? What will express my authentic creative essence?
- *Celebration*: What new form am I making, or who am I becoming? Am I embracing or resisting my full radiant expression?
- *Restoration*: How can I bring my full nature into daily acts of tending my creations? How will this inspiration change me?

Being creative is a spiritual path for keeping company with spirit. Walking the creative/spiritual path involves trusting spirit's directions. You cannot accelerate the pace of spirit unfolding. Rather than looking for external results in a particular outcome or form, it is important to remember that each stage of the creative process is vital for being with spirit. Enter into the rhythm of the present moment rather than focusing on the final outcome or creation. Spirit naturally moves between the opposite energies of expansion and retreat in a way that brings both inspiration and restoration. When a creative goal is not being realized as you intend, return to your awareness of the greater cycles and movements of spirit. Matching your energy to the guidance or flow of spirit ensures the robust health of your creations and yourself.

In the creative process, be aware of a tendency either to retain control of your creations or to give up ownership altogether. Conscious creation is a delicate relationship between holding on to and letting go of what you create. Holding on to a creation while it is developing, by following the direction of the creative flow, is what allows it to build into something meaningful. But holding on to a creation when it is long finished, or because you are trying to give it energy that is not naturally there, will only hamper your ability to move into the next creative cycle. Intentional creatives do not need to hold on to their creations because they are nourished by the creative current and the completion of each creative cycle.

Reclaim your creative essence and recognize it as a connection to the sacred. Align yourself with creative rhythms and cycles of flow as a way of keeping company with spirit. Let the creative journey redefine your experience of this precious life so you can embody your whole potential. By understanding your creative practice as a spiritual one, you redirect your creative abilities toward giving expression to your soul. As each of us reclaims this inherently soulful creativity, we will reorient the culture at large, which relies on the creative energies we put toward positive, life-enhancing ways of being—including being with spirit.

SIX

Making a Creative Life

"You don't have to prove anything," my mother said.
"Just be ready for what God sends."
—WILLIAM STAFFORD, "THE WAY IT IS"

I have told my story about meeting an eagle at the river's edge, but there is more to tell and more medicine to share. In story-based cultures, it is understood that the stories themselves have medicine for those listening. And the medicine becomes more potent in the telling over time or in the sharing of particular details. Stories are held and even details are held, the medicine given only to certain individuals at discrete times, so the energy within the story is retained or dispersed as needed.

Deva Daricha, a healer from Australia, relays, "Shamans have always told stories. One of their major ways of teaching has been to share their own experience in story. Stories of journeys through time into other dimensions; travels in consciousness beyond this life, into the realms of the dying and the dead; stories of learning the process of remembrance, of coming into being, remembering who we are, where we came from, why we are here, and where we are going."[21]

Beyond seeing the eagle, part of the story medicine in my experience at the ocean involved my journey to arrive there. My first book,

Wild Feminine, contained information to bridge the spirit–body connection related to the vagina and pelvic bowl, and, more deeply, to illuminate the places where we had lost touch with the feminine. When it initially could not find a publisher, even through a prominent literary agent, I was discouraged. But beyond the disappointment of not having a place to publish the book, my deeper discouragement arose from the growing awareness that perhaps even the women editors who held the keys to the publishing world had embodied the fractured spirit–body pattern themselves. They would not have an inner framework to comprehend the book's offerings.

Unsure of how to solve a problem that seemed insurmountable, I returned to the core of my passions to reconnect with my own creative flow. For me, this included mothering my children, writing, working with the beauty of the female body, and finding solace in nature. When my second son was a few months old and the rawness of the closed publishing door had faded to a duller sense of loss, we went in search of the wild.

I sat on the sand with my children, feeling weary. I could not imagine giving up publishing this book and what I knew to be a profoundly needed resource, but I also had no idea how to continue writing a book that might not even be published. I had two young children, and my days were filled with routine mothering tasks. How could I write and then try to publish on my own when even the simplest household tasks went unaccomplished in the nonlinear path of tending young children? Also, my faith had wavered; how would I tell my children to follow their dreams when following mine had led to such disappointment?

As I called out to spirit with these questions in my heart, the river began to drum rhythmically against the shore. The wild was talking to us, but I had no idea how to interpret its message. Then a hush descended, and the eagle flew past. In that moment, I felt a connection to the entire landscape in the core of my being, and it revealed a deeper framework that unified everything. I had a sense of complete peace, as if all of my questions had been answered; though, in actuality, very little had changed. I still had no idea how to proceed, but I had an inner calm that opened a sense of potential—the potential of the wild creative. Nature does not try to be creative; she just creates as a continual flow. In the quiet, I heard a message: *Just write*. I questioned back: *What if I finish the book and cannot find a publisher?* Again I heard, *Just write*.

Insights as Design Plans

Not long after returning from our trip to the beach, I began teaching the workshop framework, outlined in chapter 5, that came to me instead of the guidance I was seeking: *invitation, preparation, inspiration, celebration*, and *restoration*. Since what I had received seemed like a potentially valuable framework for living creatively (where typically there is no framework), I turned my attention toward teaching. Once I understood this framework for creative cycles, I could see that I was only at the beginning of the cycle in regard to my book project. What seemed like an end point with publishing houses was really a shift into the second rhythm, or preparation movement with spirit.

Going to the natural world and calling to spirit was the beginning of my own preparation. Listening to the energy currents in nature and teaching the workshop series about realigning with this flow were the essential healing I needed to continue writing and bring this work into a book form. The personal energetic work I did—restoring my connection to this deeper movement with spirit—greatly expanded my writing and created a whole body of work. Taking the long way deepened my offering and my understanding of the body–energy interface in the creative field.

In time, I realized that I had initially made a common, fundamental mistake in regard to creative dreams: I had expected the publishers or my agent or someone else outside me to make my dreams come true.

Once the first round of publishers did not take my manuscript, I discovered this truth: no one could make my dreams come true but me. Even beyond publishing a book, which I considered the pinnacle of my dream, there is the ongoing work of marketing and bringing it to an audience. Publishing a book, or holding any physically manifested creation, is something to celebrate; but like many of life's events, it is not the end point of the dream. It is a step on the journey of dream making that is taken by walking each day in the energy of one's creative center. To live from that inner radiance, we must recognize that our potential lies not with a particular creation (and its success or failure) but with the unfolding creative essence within. Dreams are not something that we place into the hands of others; rather, we look to our dreams to reflect the luminescence of our own creative energy.

Upon reclaiming my dream, I turned my attention back to the creative flow and writing. With my focus shifted from seeking a publisher, I responded instead to the workshop framework for how to read creative cycles. Teaching the class and continuing to write the manuscript would take me through the next few years and several creative cycles. Each time I taught my workshop, a powerful energy current arose in the process. And the creative current from each class further propelled the book I was writing into full form.

Then one spring, my book was done; and as it so happened, a participant in my class had connections in the publishing world. She recommended a simple way to self-publish online. With relative ease, I found my way to an editor, then a book designer, and finally an artist for the cover. I took each step as it came and self-published my first book.

Years earlier, I could have tried to force the outcome by pursuing other publishers. Instead—after receiving a deeper creative current from the wild—I made my way by following my passions and the insights that led me toward teaching, writing, and mothering. In doing so, I was richly fed while the creative process helped me redefine my inner framework to better align with my creative channel. These were the blueprints for not only finishing my creative dream of writing a book but also for developing my professional and personal life. Meanwhile, the greater energy currents that support the feminine became stronger. When my inner framework was ready, the actual publishing came first as a self-published book and then with a major publishing house. There was also permission to unleash my creative potential, which I had previously sought from a publisher; ultimately, I had to give this permission to myself. Taking the extended creative route, it was if I had hiked the trail instead of being driven there. I gained the rewards of the expanded journey in my energy field and a deep creative flow to sustain me.

And this is why, without hesitation, I can encourage you to follow your dreams and stay in touch with the wild creative that will inspire the elongated path—and inadvertently, make for a whole and brilliant life.

Full-Spectrum Creativity

Though we may perceive creativity as just a single artistic talent or gift, in actuality, people living vibrant lives share a common characteristic: a broad-based creativity that is universally applied to all facets of life. As the director of Salmon-Safe, an environmental organization that works to inspire farmers to restore habitat and protect water quality, my husband, Dan, engages creativity on a daily basis—from forming a new partnership to expand programs in British Columbia to working with a whole array of businesses and landowners. He also works with environmentally innovative farmers who see themselves as both the stewards of the land and the marketers who grow and creatively sell what they produce on the land.

One of these inspired farmers, named Diane, is a Salmon-Safe-certified flower grower in Washington's Skagit River Valley, north of Seattle. She is a lifelong creative and artist who farms with her husband, Dennis. Diane learned how to farm over decades by growing her skills out of a passion for gardening. On only seven acres (which, by most farm standards, is a small parcel of land), she has been able to grow a high-value crop of flowers by learning about the growing patterns on her land in relationship to microweather patterns. Through trial and error, and creative land management, she has discovered which flowers thrive where, learning more about the land in the process. By tending her Skagit Flats land in Puget Sound through several growing seasons, she has developed the means to work with seasonal patterns of flower growing on her particular seven acres.

Diane is in the vanguard of a revolution in re-envisioning the US cut-flower market. In the midst of what has become an unsustainable product in the marketplace, she produces local, organic cut flowers and locates the demand for them. Most cut flowers in US stores are imported, typically grown in Colombia or Ecuador—potentially on fields laden with pesticides and with no regard for workers or local ecology—and then shipped north by air. While some farms have better growing practices than others, there is little oversight. In contrast, Diane grows flowers without toxic pesticides or fertilizers, and with land management practices that ensure the health of the watershed and the river that runs near her property. She offers the value of being close to the marketplace, thus conserving transportation resources, and has also set aside a third of the land for wildlife.

Diane's creative inspiration does not stop with growing flowers and land stewardship; she saw the need to build a high-value regional market as a more sustainable way to access buyers. She seeks to raise awareness and build a market for the local flower-farming heritage. Looking to other emerging models for regional markets, Diane led the creation of a wholesale cut-flower market in Seattle, Washington. And her model for sustainability in growing flowers extends beyond the land to include partnering with other farmers. Diane realized that it was essential to work with like-minded flower growers to be able to sell together in wholesale. As a visionary, she conceived of a new model for this work she calls her "passion business," but she also envisions inspiring other growers to join the movement and work cooperatively as the way of the future.

Diane's passion for bringing people together in beneficial ways is how my husband met her. She co-organized a national conference for sustainable flower growers, wrote grants, and received funding; and she exudes the can-do cooperative vibration of a person living in her creative flow, even while tackling operational tasks far beyond farming. Diane knows where the value is and how to leverage that value. As she told Tilth Producers of Washington, "Perceive yourself as being of value, and sell yourself that way."[22] Though Diane was referencing farmers understanding the value of their products, this sage advice applies to anyone.

Follow a model like Diane, who carries a full-spectrum, broad-based creative currency: she perceives more instead of less, potential in place of lack, beauty as a purpose of its own, and opportunity even where no one else seems to, which is all rooted in her background as an artist. When I talked with her about creativity, she said, "I have often thought about how much better our shared government and community systems might be working if we did a better job of valuing, nourishing, and fostering creative leadership in our culture—starting with funding arts in schools." As she said of herself and her husband, "As artists, we are comfortable renovating a completely new area . . . We say to ourselves, 'Yes, let's go where no one has gone for a long time.'"[23]

What models of broad-based creativity can you find?

How might you expand your creative currency to have a broader application?

What new direction might you apply creative energy toward?

Passion Around the Problem

Jeremy Stoppelman is the visionary behind Yelp, a website and app product that allows users to rate businesses online and share personal reviews. The site helps thousands of people discover fabulous local eateries, especially when they're from out of town. Stoppelman came up with the concept of Yelp while attending Harvard Business School, when he became sick and searched for a doctor online. He realized that the internet contained basic contact information, but was missing any personal or word-of-mouth referrals.

In an interview with the *Wall Street Journal*, he stated that his focus has always been "passion around the problem." Not only is Stoppelman interested in bringing information to the task of problem solving, he actively brings passion to the table—namely giving a place for the expression of passion in order to direct the flow of business. As for using passion as the basis for a powerful business model, Stoppelman shares another benefit of following one's own passion: "Nothing is more rewarding than charting your own course." Though he is referring to the fate of his company, those wise words express the power of harnessing your creative energy and directing its flow in your life.[24]

Closer to home, I observed an example of the power of engaging "passion around the problem" in the evolution of our local grade school. When we moved into the neighborhood a few years before having children of our own, the local school was declining. Enrollment was sharply down, and there were scarcely enough kids to keep the doors open. The neighborhood was undergoing a renaissance, but the school's tired-looking 1920s structure had a derelict feel.

We had two young children when we heard that a vibrant environmental education program for middle school students was looking for a new home and considering moving into this school. As neighbors of the possible new venture, we actively campaigned, including speaking to the school board, to have the program located at our school.

The environmental special-focus program—the brainstorm of a local midwife and activist mother, Sarah Taylor—was created to bring middle school students into the wild and create an active culture of environmental and community service. The founders were looking to expand their groundbreaking and successful program to its own school building. Thus, Sunnyside Environmental School became our neighborhood school.

As a family, we were thrilled to have this dynamic program drop right into the center of our lives, but more fascinating was the transformation that took place. The local school went from being a neglected building with faded lawns to a thriving series of gardens filled with native plants and edibles—all along the entire perimeter of the campus. The children tended the gardens; and as the gardens thrived, so did the children. The older students traveled farther afield into the community and the wild, following a rotating series of yearlong themed curricula: river, mountain, and forest. And the neighborhood benefited from the overflowing abundance of a thoughtfully tended energy field. Within two years, the once weed-filled ground around the school supported layers of blossoming plants, offering cool shade and a fragrant respite from the urban landscape. Now when I pass by the school, I naturally slow my pace and breathe more deeply. My body responds to the well-tended space and sense of the wild before I consciously register its presence.

The newfound vibrancy at the school site attracted new families to the neighborhood, and just as the gardens bloomed, within two years, the school's numbers swelled beyond capacity. Murals were painted, classrooms were renovated to make more room, the library reopened, and the auditorium was restored. With a functioning auditorium, the children began each day by singing together in a raucous event called "Warble and Chirp" for the younger students and "Morning Meeting" for the older ones. The school similarly attracted creative teachers, and every room teemed with colorful projects and animated children. Just as we'd seen with the blooming gardens, we witnessed magic moving from one creative individual and unfolding into a thousand reflections.

From our vantage point as neighbors, we observed the school's profound transformation. Once our children entered the school, however, we saw another level of these creative wheels in motion. Sarah Taylor had developed an environmental curriculum because it was the type of hands-on education she wanted to see, but her creative vision was also integrated through every aspect of the school. She set the precedent for a dynamic art, music, and gardening curriculum by asking the parenting and local community to invest, making use of student teachers and AmeriCorps volunteers. She cocreated the curriculum with the teachers, encouraging refinement as they learned how best to engage the children at different age levels. She sought donations and volunteers in order to remodel classrooms and restore the school and its grounds, each project inspired by her creative ingenuity. And in between all of these projects, she managed to midwife the births of many babies, some of whom later attended the school. Taylor's creative energy truly seemed to have no limits.

Taylor retired from her position as the school's principal after eight years of onsite and curriculum development, staying long enough to ensure the program's long-term success. Even now, when not volunteering as a midwife in Haiti or working on one of her other "retirement" projects, Taylor occasionally comes back to visit the school.

One day, I saw her roaming the halls, connecting with students and teachers alike. I asked her what advice she would give for others to live creatively, and she replied, "You can't be afraid of the obstacles. If you see an obstacle, say to yourself, 'That's not really an obstacle.' Then find a way around it. And there will be messes—things won't be perfect. But don't let that stop you . . . Look for the beauty." Then she told a story about a time at Sunnyside when a father came to her because he did not have the money to send his child on the special eighth-grade field trip to Catalina Island. (Talking with her often involved listening to a story, because her life was rich in experiences.) Always ready to apply someone's skills to a task at hand, she discovered that he painted murals. Taylor suggested that he paint a beautiful mural for the school, and then they would find the funds for his child's trip. She pointed at the wall in the lunchroom as she spoke, where a multihued mural spread across one whole side. I had seen that mural for years without knowing the story behind it. It was a perfect example of how Taylor built a thriving school one creative step at a time.

The Creative Key: Identifying and Addressing a Valued Need

Creative energy can be inspiring, but creative success is determined by one key: defining and meeting a clear need. Sarah Taylor's environmental school was a success because of her creative vision, but even more so because she identified a valuable need for a type of education that aligned with what many other families desired. She also identified the need for more creative energy in schools, both in how they are run (so teachers can be more creative) and how students are engaged in the learning process.

In another example of applying creative energy to a specific need, architect Ben Kaiser used his creative skills to address the significant and present need for earthquake retrofitting in schools. Many older schools are built from brick, the least earthquake-resistant material; retrofitting these schools is structurally challenging and costly. But Kaiser had a solution: place strong steel cages in hallways by fitting them through holes in the roof. This adds structural support and "safety zones" where students can gather—at one-quarter of the price of typical seismic upgrade retrofits. Kaiser's plan addresses two key needs: the need for simple retrofit solutions and the need for low-cost solutions that schools can afford. His plan could save millions of dollars and countless lives.[25]

There are numerous examples in business where the most successful ventures apply creative thinking to real needs and services; people pay for what is valuable to them. Jack Dorsey's inventions of Twitter and Square addressed a need for streamlining the delivery of information and payment processing, respectively. Apple is often referenced as the leading example of an organizational culture of creative innovation that is transformative in the marketplace. Steve Jobs had his engineers sign the interiors of the first Apple computers, feeling strongly that he and his team were artists creating a new art form.

Being a therapist who works on the body, I recognize the importance of maintaining core body warmth. For years, in the cold, wet winters of the Pacific Northwest (where I live), I had difficulty staying warm in my core until I envisioned a short wool skirt made of recycled fabric. I contacted Karina, an artisan in my hometown of Portland, Oregon, who repurposes shirts and hats from salvaged sweaters and materials; this is both creative outlet and a business that works well with her family life as the mother of three daughters. A fan of her hats, I suggested she create the short sweater-skirt. Karina made a first batch of them from sweaters of all colors, highlighting them with her characteristic bird or flower designs (made from recycled fabrics). I purchased four of them, and she went on to successfully market this new product as a "hip wrap." Karina's hip wraps layer fashionably over jeans too, which serve the needs for both warmth and style. They can be spotted on many trendy creatives around town, and they have added a dynamic product to Karina's clothing line.

In every arena, success is there to be had when an unmet need is identified and addressed to provide value. Alternative practitioners represent a rapidly growing segment of the healthcare business because they provide the holistic care missing from mainstream medicine. Starbucks created an iconic brand by identifying a need for making consistently high-quality coffee more available in every neighborhood. In the same vein, local coffee businesses like Portland's Stumptown Coffee Roasters created a niche market for customers who sought a more local and independent coffee source. If you see a need in your community that is not being addressed, you have likely discovered a business opportunity or a potential way to generate revenue.

What needs can you identify in the various aspects of your life?

How might creative energy be applied to address these needs?
Where can you identify a need that could become a place of value?

Drawing Upon the Creative Community

When I was nineteen and living in Mexico as a university student with my dear friend, Sara, we climbed aboard a bus heading to a traditional festival of *Dia de los Muertos*, or Day of the Dead, in a village called Tzintzuntzán. Being young and open to the spirit of adventure, we left without considering where we would spend the night. Arriving in a dusty village square after a long bus ride, we found that all lodging in the village was full because of the festival. Out of options, Sara and I decided to spend the night in the cemetery where the festival was taking place. We stepped away from the limitation of no rooms into the potential of a cemetery filled with villagers. Because we were so young, it didn't occur to us that we might be intruding on a cultural ritual. But I am glad for that innocence; I can still smell the fragrance of that place of tended earth and spirit all these years later.

As night was descending, we walked to the graveyard. The warmth of spirit emanated from the arbor entry covered in bright orange marigolds and the path of petals that led to it. We followed, entranced by a palpable, soft energy that I imagined came from taking such good care of ancestors—something I had never witnessed at home. We passed through the floral doorway that signaled a crossing of the threshold, and walked among the earthen mounds that were covered with food prepared for the dead. Simple white candles made pools of light for families as they sat together, the children eating and some already drifting toward sleep. The sleeping children were wrapped in shawls and tucked against the earthen mounds as if the graves were pillows. Far from the notion of a haunted cemetery, it was a place to rest, eat, pray, or catch up with friends. Perhaps our cultural idea of a haunted graveyard comes from our lack of care—the forgotten intersection between life, death, and the realm of spirit.

Only years later did I begin to understand how alive the graveyard was on that night of *Dia de los Muertos*. It pulsed with energy, like the life force that pours through the womb at birth. Of course, birth and death are intimately connected as two parts of the creative cycle, but it was a realization for me that tending to spirit in response to death is regenerative. Among the graves that night was a deeply feminine presence in the dark, earthen tending of food and the flowers on the graves. For an outsider, this might have seemed like a quaint ritual—perhaps valuable for its folk-art altars and creations, but not more than decorative. And yet, in the process of this ritual of tending, an energy had risen to meet us. This was the energy of spirit, of all life—the energy of the potential form, the return to spirit, and the yet-to-be-born creative life force. Spirit comes to places that are tended.

It was cold that night, and Sara and I had worn only the lightest jackets. As the night deepened and the candles were blown out, we huddled together. We were surrounded by the village families and, in the openness of our youth, did not even register a separation. Neither did they, it seemed, although I am certain we were a strange sight—two young *gringas* shivering together. Where had we come from? Where were our families? Someone built a fire near us, and a blanket was passed for us to use. We lay in the womb of this graveyard, feeling very much alive. In the dawn light, the villagers rose like shadows to sing. The energy of that song wove its way into my soul, the very food that our creative essence requires. May we always remember to give ourselves the energy contained in a ritual such as *Dia de los Muertos*, so we may rise and create with spirit.

Being creative together as a community is profoundly regenerative. The interface of spirit and body in an annual ritual like *Dia de los Muertos* nourishes the community soul. Likewise, working as a community is a reminder that you don't need to rely solely upon your own resources or create everything you need. Recognize the creative resources amid the greater community, and draw from this expanded creative potential. You can receive energy from your community (or from exploring a new community, as in the story I just related) or collaborate with others to enhance your creative reach or skill set. For example, while I am thankful for technology as a tool, it is not naturally intuitive for me. So I have sought out community members who have helped me grow my business and share my work with an increasingly global and web-based audience. And I have witnessed how the creative essence is powerfully regenerated in collective events and rituals. Ponder your own community and the resources in the creative collective.

What creative resources are present in your community?

How might these community resources assist your creative potential?

What opportunities are there for you to be creative in a collective manner?

Take Your Creative Currency to the Bank

Creative energy is the new currency for passionate living, and is the foundation for many entrepreneurial ventures and successful products. Beekeeper Brad Swift is the founder of Portland Bee Balm, a handcrafted lip balm made primarily from beeswax that he harvests in his backyard. With an eye for creativity, I am intrigued by inspired business ventures. I first saw Swift's lip balm at my local health-food store, and then an interview with him in the local paper caught my attention.

Initially, Swift was working as a teacher, but after being introduced to beekeeping by a friend, Swift thought it would be fun to try it. He liked working with his hands because he grew up helping his father install and refinish wood floors. He first established hives to produce honey but also wound up with beeswax, which makes a good wood finish and waterproofing paste. One day, he tried making lip balm for his girlfriend; soon he made more for friends. It was popular, and he decided to start a business producing it for health-food stores, handcrafting his own small wooden displays. Swift's creative venture proved to be profitable. Within a few months of sales, he had made up his initial $1,500 investment in materials. Seven months later, he quit his job as a teacher because he was already exceeding his previous salary. He is doing something he is passionate about that allows him to express his creativity: that is real money in the bank.[26]

Any career will receive a boost from creative thinking, and creativity is increasingly called upon to integrate work and home, or build a life that has room for our dreams and self-expression in the midst of making a living. Once again, the creative flow provides guidance for how to integrate inspiration with the ability to generate an income. For example, my husband thrives in his work leading on-the-ground implementation of sustainable land-management practices in the Northwest while using various aspects of his background and skills. But when funding for his environmental nonprofit was scarce (through the traditional nonprofit model of foundation grants), he found a new flow of funding by developing fee-based consulting services that leveraged the organization's expertise and mission. Look for the direction of flow in your life or business in order to transform creative flow into your currency for living.

Energy Session: It's Not about the Creations but Living in the Flow

When Jessie came for an energy session, she was seeking creative inspiration. Several years earlier, as a passionate young musician, she had recorded a CD. This initial CD was fairly successful and expanded her opportunities to perform. But then a follow-up CD sold poorly, and she began questioning herself. Over time, Jessie found that the pressure to be a commercial success inhibited her creative expression, and she struggled with playing music at all. Anyone who has ever experienced a project, relationship, or dream not being received in the manner hoped for can relate to this sense of failure that may inhibit future expressions.

When I brought Jessie's attention to her energy center, there was no sense of energy movement, only a pattern of stagnation. I asked her to think about her current CD, and the stagnant pattern was accentuated. Jessie's energy revealed how she was internalizing the outer response to her music. We talked further and realized she was holding on to her glimpse of past success in music—as if it held the key to her future success—instead of moving forward into the energy of the present. Being creative over time requires being open to whatever happens, and even being prepared to fail in some way; that is, to create something without expectations of a certain outcome. Any form of expression carries inherent risk. We must be willing to share what we create with others in order for it to be fully realized. However, the true value lies in our *willingness* to be creative rather than external with our response to our creation. We never know the full impacts our creations may have over time.

In doing healing work for others, I have found this practice of creative detachment essential. To be effective as a healer, I hold a neutral space. I remain unattached to any particular direction of the treatment or healing in order to receive the purest flow of energy to the greatest benefit of the individual. This neutral presence is what allows for the divine or greater field to guide the way instead of being limited to the human perspective.

Remaining in contact with the creative-energy current and allowing the flow to guide each creation enables a person to be infinitely creative. And the abundance and creative potential in this broader field has applications for all aspects of life. Holding on to any particular creation as a form of validation (or for some other reason) only restricts creative flow. A person may hold on to prior successes, creations, relationships, jobs, ways of working, and patterns of being that no longer serve them, partly in fear that there is a shortage of good things coming to them. However, by letting go of the particulars, they hold on to the creative flow instead, ultimately receiving what is needed in a way that more readily matches each point in time.

For Jessie, I encouraged her to breathe the attachment to her first success down into the earth as a form of energetic release. She could still remember the excitement and feeling of having made a successful product, but she had to release her attachment to the response others had to her previous creation. By releasing the hold on this creation, Jessie allowed the creative energy to move through her, propelling past creative works into new forms and guiding her future work.

After Jessie released the energy of her first CD, I invited her to bring her second CD into the creative field and see that it was as essential to her creative process as the first one. Instead of judging its worth by the marketplace response, she could notice the way it affected her creative evolution. When Jessie saw this recording in a different light, energy pulsed through her center. I asked if she could feel the energy flow returning to her core, as this core creative place was where she was meant to keep her focus. By maintaining focus on her creative center, Jessie could be creatively fulfilled, allowing her creations to come into form without an agenda about what they would bring or achieve.

Sometimes artists or creative visionaries are at the forefront of consciousness, and the audience to receive the work has not yet arrived. When they connect to their creative center, the nourishment comes from within rather than depending on an outside reception. Returning to that center can give artists the nurturing they need to keep going while the rest of the world catches up. It also ensures that they themselves are cherished as much as what they create. Creativity is perhaps even more of a personal evolution than it is a means of making something of value; and when this is understood, the process of what to value changes. Jessie realized that she was using creativity in her music but not really including her own self in the process. The creative channel is meant to nourish us, not just our creations.

Counter to external messages, there is no scarcity of energy in the creative flow. The creative field grows stronger with each creative work, and in the release of each creation, has a greater capacity for creative flow—as long as the creative cycle is completed by allowing the full birth process and release. Sometimes a fear of loss—that what was made will never be found again—keeps someone holding on to what was created. And it is true that what was made is unique and will never be repeated exactly. Yet the creative current is always there, carrying new energy and fresh potential with all that is needed for the next creative evolution.

Apply Creative Energy to Build Creative Currency

Creative energy has applications for all aspects of your life. Take a moment to see where your creative energy is already abundant and where you could use more. Find new ways to express your creativity and enrich your energy flow. With creative energy moving, you restore currency for reinvesting in your life.

Once upon a time, creativity was an everyday part of homemaking, from growing food to tending the land to making clothing, sustaining a whole way of living. Now knitting and sewing, canning, and cooking can be more hobby than necessity, yet taking care of the home generates potent energy.

Relationships benefit tremendously from an investment of creative energy. Particularly when sustaining a long-term relationship or friendship, being creative about how you connect or make time for one another sustains and revitalizes the connection. Be romantic and spontaneous in your marriage or partnership. Take a trip to a new place, explore a new part of town, or take an art or dance class together. Even with a hectic schedule, you can do simple things to surprise your partner, like with a chocolate bar or a fresh latte—something you know will be appreciated. You can do the same for a friend or colleague, or even yourself. Being creative and creatively expressive brings fresh energy to any moment.

With respect to intimate relationships, creativity and sex are both related to the energy movement in the lower chakras. If one aspect of this energy space is flowing, the other may be more energized as well. Likewise, if a person feels creatively frustrated, they may experience a diminished libido. Frustration with sex or a sexual partner can cause creative stagnation as well. In the face of sexual frustration, try being creative and see what new inspirations arise. Notice how your creative energy and sexual energy are related.

Even when you are challenged by one area that seems to be lacking or blocked creatively, restoring the flow in a broader way can stimulate an overall creative resurgence. When you find yourself blocked, work with the creative energy in the areas that are flowing to draw upon your overall creative range.

Exercise: Illuminating the Facets of Your Creative Life
Find a quiet place with a pad of paper and a pen.

- Make a creative wheel. Modeling the wheel on the example on the next page, label each section with the various aspects of your life (such as home, work, money/abundance, partnerships, creative expression, health, sexuality, parenting, spirituality).

Reflecting on one section at a time, answer the questions below to gain insight into the many dimensions of your creative life.

- How do you (or could you) use creativity in each area?
- In which facets do you feel a vibrant connection to the creative flow?
- How is this reflected in your creative currency and abundance?
- Where do you feel creatively stagnant or frustrated?
- How might you apply creativity to restore the creative abundance in all of these aspects? Where are you in need of more creative flow or creative collaboration?

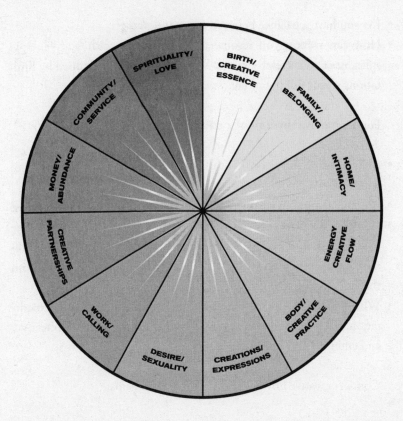

Think about these aspects in terms of "The Body's Creative-Energy Field" diagram (page 37):

- Is there a relationship between energy/inspiration and physical/form?
- If not, what needs more structure/form and what needs more energy/ inspiration?
- Are there core creative patterns/structures you want to change or redefine?
- Is any lacking aspect in need of more left (feminine) or more right (masculine) field energy flow? Are your masculine and feminine fields working in alignment?

- Do you have a balance between *being* and *doing*?
- How can working on resonance or alignment with body/energy/spirit assist your creative range? Where is your range defined by limitations versus full potential?

Ponder the five rhythms of a creative cycle:

- Are you being intentional with your creative energy in all aspects of your life?
- Are you taking your creativity through full cycles in these various areas?
- Compare the places of creative flow versus stagnation: Do they relate to completion of cycles? Where might you move through full creative cycles in new areas? How can you receive and take action from the guidance of your center?
- Where might you increase connection to spirit through ritual, meditation, nature, or some other way to further express your wild creative, and embody your radiant energy field?

Connect creative flow to manifesting your dreams:

- What are your fullest dreams in each of these areas?
- Where are you in touch with these dreams?
- How can creativity help realize these dreams?

Live the Wild Creative: The Art of Resonance

The essential point in being creative is to live the wild creative—to live in connection to the pulse of life. We do this by tending each soul-filled creation until it stands on its own, following the channel of our life flow. We give our children and our creations to the world and then focus on the current that is moving through to guide our next creative movement. We come into resonance with the creative flow itself.

The Wild Creative Process

I recently came across an interview by entertainment writer Jake Coyle with actor Javier Bardem, who had just finished his largest film role yet as the villain in the James Bond movie *Skyfall*. Bardem had already received wide acclaim from his acting peers and won an Oscar while still in his thirties. Initially hesitant to take on a more constraining role in a blockbuster movie, Bardem was pleased to find it was a "very creative process."

Interestingly, Bardem goes on to describe the "creative process" rather than the specific role, indicating his awareness of the creative flow that gives shape to the character rather than the other way around. Bardem reveals another aspect of staying connected to flow (rather than to a specific character or creation)—the willingness to be vulnerable that it requires: "It's always about really dismantling what you think you know and the security and the safety zone where you are, trying to make a step forward to something new, something that will put you in some trouble."[27]

The creative force moving through you into a visible form of expression is the ultimate sense of exhilaration. Maintaining the focus on the creative process means that you are free to express this energy and less likely to limit its expression based on the responses of others to that creation. When we create, energy moves and gives us a tangible sense of being alive. Likewise, our creations have lives of their own that are confined only by our focus on the discreet moments they represent in time.

If we focus on the flow, not only do we have more creative freedom ourselves but our creations are more likely to find the energy to support them. Trying to control what we create results in more challenges than simply working with the quality and flow of energy in our creative process. By focusing on the process of creating something—a piece of art, a performance, a connection with someone, a relationship, an alignment in the body—the creation is infused with this greater potential.

Cultivating the Resonance of Your Center

When a series of chords are played out of sync with one another, their physical vibrations make a dissonance. If instead they are played in alignment, they create a harmonic frequency, or a resonance. Being able to thrive creatively requires setting up and maintaining a harmonic frequency of spirit, energy, and body within your center—further drawing on the divine, universal energy field to amplify this potential.

Our bodies and energy fields can achieve resonance, and resonance in your center can be cultivated. It is the most powerful tool I know for changing your energy field from a congested to a regenerative state. But stress, doubt, and worry tend to constrict the energy field or disrupt energy alignment. In contrast, spending time in nature, being creative, sharing love, tending your home, and taking care of your body all create resonance in the energy field.

Begin to notice your own relationship with resonance. Observe your body–energy response to stress—like that of a loud city intersection, for example. When you focus your attention on the effects, you may find that your body is tense or your energy field is compressed. Your breathing may be shallow or you may hold your breath. You may feel tightness in your chest or have a furrowed brow. Some experiences of stress may be so common that you have learned to ignore the response in your body. Compare your response to a congested intersection with your response to a well-designed urban space. Take note of how the resonance or dissonance of the place affects your well-being.

In contrast to stress patterns that disrupt resonance, pay attention to what supports and aligns your energy. Notice how your body feels after a yoga class or after spending time with a good friend. Work in the garden and touch the earth, or go to a wild place and observe the changes in your body and energy: your body relaxes and your breath becomes more full; your energy softens and expands. By noticing these effects, you can better cultivate a practice of resonance in your own center and nurture it on a daily basis.

Energy Practices for Resonance

Resonance is supported by energy practices that invite and create core alignment, such as visualization or meditation, engaging the creative flow, and, for those with the inclination, attuning to the divine through ritual or prayer (like "Making a Spiritual Bath" on page 106). Listening to beautiful music or visiting an art exhibit—particularly one with refined pieces—can also facilitate resonance in the creative field. Feeling the connection to your loved ones or calling to mind specific things for which you are grateful creates resonance. If your sense of the sacred is found in nature, making routine pilgrimages to the wild will align you as well. Experiment with the power of blessings. For example, *May I be blessed, May I be held, May I receive the peace of my center*, spoken or repeated like a mantra, cultivates the resonance and radiance of your core field.

Blessings are like a sublime piece of music: they elevate the energy around and within us. A blessing, like anything that facilitates resonance, can mitigate stress or cultivate resonance in our field in the midst of stress. When we are feeling the effects of stress, there is often a sense of fear or scarcity contracting the energy field. To alleviate these effects, use blessings or a creative practice to focus on your desired intentions (rather than on the stress), restoring the resonance within. Instead of trying to fix the sense of scarcity, address the contraction in your field by increasing resonance. Simply shift your focus from a source of stress or worry to that of intention, gratitude, or love to change the pattern in your center. For example, if you feel stressed about not having enough time or resources, focus on that stress and notice what occurs in your body and energy field. Then change your focus to an intention for yourself, such as *May I find the spaciousness in my time today*. Observe what happens in your center when you say these words, focusing on the potential instead of what is missing.

We weave our lives every day using the quality of energy that moves through our creative centers. A practice of resonance involves intentionally choosing a high vibration of energy at each moment. Louise

Hay, a prominent mind-body-spirit author, references the power of our thoughts in creating our lives. Hay says, "This is the moment when you're either enjoying or not enjoying your life. What you're feeling now is creating your tomorrows. Isn't that a wonderful thing to know? You are in charge of your life."[28] Every thought is a magnet for energy and a chance to choose resonance over dissonance, creative engagement over resignation. Thoughts such as "I'm stressed" or "I'm tired" can be changed to "I'm blessed" or "May I receive what I need." Shifting our focus away from the burden of all the tasks yet to be accomplished and toward the magic potential within each day radically shifts not only the lens we are looking through but the energy framework with which we encounter the day ahead of us.

An antidote for frustration or scarcity in any moment or aspect of your life is to instead ponder what you are thankful for or what you love. Observe your energy field in the presence of frustration and then notice how it changes when you shift your focus to the capacity of your abundance; perhaps you feel a sense of more space and capacity that in fact gives you an infusion of energy resources. When you work with resonance in your own field by using the energy medicine from blessings, ritual, pure presence, going to the wild, or the like, the feeling of "not enough" becomes the expansiveness of the embodied present and the mysterious beauty it contains when you are available to witness it. This practice can also re-energize your center during moments of challenge, like a traffic jam, a long line at the post office, or other times when you need it. It soothes the energy field around you and helps others (a difficult taxi driver, an irritable child, your partner during a conflict) align with your resonance, bringing extra calm when they are stressed. In finding resonance with the greater energy field, you already have more of whatever you need, including the unexpected blessings that arise when there is an opening.

Notice where resonance is best cultivated for you. Being intentionally creative through dance, movement, or other art forms cultivates resonance. We can also find resonance by spending time with loved ones and the animal companions in our lives. Pet therapy is based on the healing resonance animals provide. If you have an animal in your home, stroke your pet with intention or spend five minutes connecting together, to see what changes in your body and energy. Pay attention to the field of resonance in the home that is created by those who live there. Tending the home, doing yardwork, or sharing a meal as a household cultivates resonance in this field. Whenever a group works together for a shared purpose, resonance is established. There is the potential for resonance in creative partnerships and friendships. Our own resonance is enhanced when in the company of like-minded others, which is why group meditation or ritual is more powerful as individuals expand the field of resonance together.

I once witnessed collective resonance at a Grateful Dead concert in Eugene, Oregon. I had missed the whole Deadhead scene but happened to attend one of their last concerts, held at Autzen Stadium. The band was playing, and the notes seemed discordant, when suddenly the sound and the whole field of the crowd came into a profound shared resonance, aligning as if one. The Grateful Dead were one of those rare musical groups that could achieve this with an audience.

Discover whatever cultivates resonance for you, both as an individual and with those around you. Make it a priority to inhabit a field of resonance, and reach for your go-to ways to find resonance whenever you are feeling out of alignment in your center.

Energy Session: Moving from Reaction to Resonance

Lisa came for a session because she felt successful in her career but frustrated with her personal life. I invited her to notice her creative center and, in doing so, discovered an imbalance between her right and left sides. The right, masculine side was pulsing with heat while the left, feminine side felt cold and empty. This is a common pattern for someone who has "achieved" their goals: the masculine energy field is engaged in the process of checking items off their to-do list while their inner desires are going unmet, the left energy field diminished.

I asked Lisa what her main frustration was, and she immediately answered, "Dating," noting that despite her professional success, she seemed to attract either unavailable or disrespectful partners. As she talked about this frustration, the energy of her center became compressed. Lisa wanted a partner with whom to share the lifestyle she had achieved, yet her success had not translated to her relationships. She was increasingly hesitant to date because she kept repeating the same pattern. I told her that with the way her core-energy map was contracting while she was even thinking about dating, she was more likely to energize and create her fears than her actual desires. Since energy flows through our creative field, and affects what we make and how energy comes to us, focusing on stress and difficulty in relationships will often magnify this in the outer world.

I invited Lisa to bring focus and presence to her center. Sensing her core body initially released tears and heavy grief for not finding the partnership she yearned for; but I guided her to release the grief into the earth by letting go of the heavy sensation with each exhale. After visualizing this release, she began to explore the creative energy within herself. So often, whether a person is seeking a relationship, a job, a new home, or another opportunity, I find that they hold their fear and anxiety about what they are not receiving rather than focusing on what they actually desire for themselves.

When worry or stress is held in the center, it constricts the energy field, limiting one's potential to manifest a change. This means the energy field contracts in the presence of stress rather than expanding to create potential. Although it is counterintuitive when we feel a sense of scarcity, if we hold a desire in the center of our energy field with openness and trust that it can happen, the desire's potency is strengthened in the field. Traditional Maya healer Don Elijio taught my teacher, Rosita Arvigo, that the essential part of a prayer is *I trust with all of my heart*; that trust applies to our creative dreams as well. The inner sense of trust expands our potential to the greater energy field.

I encouraged Lisa to feel her worth and inner radiance—her right to be valued—even though this was challenging for her. She understood her value theoretically, but on an energy level, she was dismissing herself and felt unworthy. As I invited Lisa to focus on her center, she remarked, "I realize that I don't even believe this is possible for me—that I'm not valuable enough for someone who would have the attributes I want." If she was not in contact with her own value, or equated her value to only outer success rather than inner worth, it would be difficult to attract a partner who could appreciate and honor her true beauty. We are likely to find alignment in the same vibration that we are holding. Since many times what we hold reflects old patterns or family-of-origin creative imprints and maps, this is where we must do our work to change what we create.

Lisa explored this inner landscape and saw her own radiance in a new way. Then she set an intention for the type of person she was seeking. She imagined the energy and essence of this person, and the feeling of their connection. I asked her if there was currently anything besides a partner that she wanted in her life. She wanted to travel to Australia, but found that she often stopped herself before she even started to plan the trip because she did not know where to stay or the details of how it would work. I suggested that, instead of the masculine aspect that likes to know everything, she invite her feminine aspect to imagine what she desired and be open to the potential of a trip. The feminine invites us into the unknown mystery, and we need our feminine energy running to receive the unexpected gifts that may come as a result. As soon as she imagined what was possible, her left side began to pulse with energy. She saw the potential of exploring new ground and felt the first sensations of passion and excitement in her being.

By allowing and responding to the movement of new energy via her feminine creative side, Lisa could reinspire the masculine forms in her life. Even though she might have to move through the resistance of needing to know all details ahead of time, taking a trip could also appeal to the masculine sense of adventure. I recommended that Lisa make a commitment to daily visualizations for surrounding herself with loving energy, setting intentions for what she wanted in a partner and for herself. In this way, she would be more likely to draw this type of person to her and send clearer energy signals when meeting others. She had been thinking about filling out an online dating form, and I suggested she become crystal clear in her energy before engaging that process—to energize her desires rather than her fears. In this way, Lisa would change the embodied pattern of her creative-energy field to reflect the resonance of potential rather than a reaction to scarcity. Her creative energy would more easily flow through this new pattern, shifting what she attracts and makes for herself as well.

Exercise: Creating a Resonant Energy Field

To cultivate resonance in your own creative field, work with this next exercise. Find a comfortable sitting position in a place of your choosing.

1. Call to mind the creative-energy field within your body. Ponder the boundaries of your body, and the interface between your body and the realms of energy and spirit.

2. Feel the base upon which you are sitting, and make a connection in your mind's eye to the vibrant earth. Notice how your physical body is connected to the earth and all the physical manifestations of your creativity. Let yourself rest into and be nourished by this connection. If you are experiencing any form of stress, release this energy into the earth. Holding the stress energy won't help you address the issue, so set down these burdens.

3. Sense the energy field around your body and the warmth that emanates from your center. Notice how this light from within is less defined than your body but is moved by your breath and intention.

Take a breath and then exhale, inviting your radiance to respond. Breathe toward each side of your creative field, engaging the feminine and masculine energies. Repeat two to three more times, inhaling fresh air and chi and then exhaling this new energy into your center. Let the energy exchange brighten each part of your energy field.

4. Imagine walking around your energy field and brushing off any heaviness or stagnant areas where the energy is restricted, smoothing out any worries, tensions, or areas of stress. In your mind's eye, walk in a full circle around yourself, brushing away or releasing what is no longer needed. Now breathe into your core energy field again and let this radiance take up even more room. When we release places of constriction, we have more energy space to create with.

5. Remember the creative dreams that you listed in the last exercise, or ponder the creative intentions that come to mind. It can be as simple as *May I embody the peace of this moment.* Place these dream seeds in the sacred center of your energy field, and feel the quality of energy they contain as the seeds of your realized dreams.

6. Now walk around your field again in your mind's eye, this time blessing your center: *I am sacred. May I receive the light of spirit. May I stand in my radiant potential.* Invite the interface with the broader realm of spirit, imagining the bright sunlight, the gentle breeze, the divine wild infusing your dream seeds with the energy to be realized. Remember the sacredness of your soul and the creative channel within, and bring this beauty into the embodied forms of your life.

Realizing a Creative Dream

One day at a networking discussion group, when I was talking about realizing a creative dream, a woman stopped me. She said, "What do you mean by a creative dream? I understand the concept of having a dream and realizing it, but what's different about a creative dream?" I paused to reflect. To me, a dream is what you want for yourself and your life; a dream goes beyond a goal and into the realm of potential and imagination. And a *creative dream* entails using your creativity to reach these further realms and bring your dreams into being.

On my list of personal dreams is a family retreat place at the beach. But with three young children, and the extensive financial and physical demands of raising a family while running a business, this seemed like a far-off and unreachable dream at first. Still, I nurture my dreams by setting yearly intentions for them. I also have a daily practice of intentionally engaging my creativity, which may be as simple as taking a walk with my senses awake or a few hours of writing time.

Last spring, I found the dream of an ocean retreat floating into my awareness, as if calling to me. Knowing the interplay between spirit and form that arises in the creative process, I paid attention to this message. Also in the spring, my son's middle school took a multiday field trip to the coast. Traveling out to chaperone his trip, I noted more for-sale signs on properties than I had seen before, and the prices were lower than in previous years. The housing market in the city had rebounded, but the coast was still lagging behind.

After the field trip, my husband and I drove to the coast for the weekend to look at some of these houses. The second house we saw that day captured our imagination. Underneath the dirt and mildew (the result of sitting vacant for years), it looked like a Jack Kerouac writing cabin. The pine walls, stone fireplace, and sun-filled rooms invited the poetic mind. Under the cobwebs were detailed period light fixtures of burnished metal and glass. A set of double French doors opened onto a courtyard, and the house could easily hold a family or two in its embrace. It needed everything from cleaning and paint to new plumbing and wiring; and it had never had a washer or dryer, let alone a dishwasher. But the potential was undeniable. We held our breath, hoping the foundation was solid, and reached for our dream.

I knew this was an *invitation*—one that likely wouldn't come again—and it had been on my list of pondered dreams for so long that it felt wrong to turn it down. We accepted the invitation to begin, and placing it into the familiar flow of creative rhythms, I knew that the next phase would be the hard work of *preparation*. This knowledge was helpful because, true to the pattern, the preparation phase contained the stress of taking on a ninety-year-old house that had never been well heated or properly plumbed and wired. It needed repairs, both expected and unexpected. More than a few times, I felt the rising sense of panic or dread that can accompany the restoration of an old house. Not to worry, though; that's part of the experience when you stretch to reach for a big dream. It's like the birthing process, when things feel overwhelming and impossible. The important dreams can involve this type of stretching in order to find form.

Amid the process of moving through the preparation phase and managing the stress of a construction project, I kept a lookout for the inevitable signs of the next phase: *inspiration*. These are the glimpses of progress or blessings received, like the luminous aura that surrounded the house in the coastal light. I made a practice of cultivating resonance, releasing the energy of stress, and blessing myself and the project to encourage energy alignment and ease.

The inspirations that arose helped me through another difficult aspect of realizing a dream: the vulnerability it entails. I felt vulnerable stretching into the new territory of standing in what had felt unreachable. It was like conceiving a pregnancy and then realizing all of the responsibility that comes with it. Coastal insurance and flooding issues, more expenses, and the complexities of managing a property from afar weren't really a part of my "dream." Also, it can be easier to strive for a dream than to actually receive it; a sense of not being worthy may be beneath the striving. I used blessings such as *May I receive this gift for my family and myself*, *May I step into the joy of this ocean retreat*, and *May I celebrate this adventure* to build a bridge from my comfort zone of striving and working toward a dream (which keeps one smaller than one's potential) to fully enjoying the dividends of creative labor.

The path to realizing creative dreams is not linear but cyclical, so there can be movement back and forth through these creative rhythms in the process of making a dream come true. There were days of blocked motion, like when the front yard had to be excavated to find old pipes and the sewer line was severed in the process. But always, we were met with unexpected blessings, such as the kindness of neighbors and strangers. For example, we went for ice cream with the boys after one long day. When I realized the shop only accepted cash, I told the boys we'd have to return another time. Just then, a woman stepped forward to pay. The boys learned the words *good Samaritan* that day. And though we went beyond the loan amount for the house in our expanding restoration project, we provided a summer of employment to gifted carpenters and a creative husband-and-wife contracting team who could do or fix anything, even down to the final detail of sewing the curtains.

There was also unexpected magic, like the day I wished for two natural-latex beds, knowing they were beyond our diminishing budget, and the local furniture store just happened to have two of them on a closeout special. Or the day when I prepared to set up rental information online and wished to talk to someone who had already done this: a knock came at my Portland door, two hours away from the coast. There was a man asking about a bed frame that was leaning against our cedar tree—a frame that someone else had left and I hadn't even seen. Together, we went out to examine it. "Yes, please take it," I said to him of the black-and-silver frame. As we loaded it onto his car and talked, it turned out he and his wife lived in the same coastal town as our beach cottage. They rented their cottage every summer and had honed the process to an art that he was happy to share.

By early fall, when the house restoration was complete, we moved furniture in and stayed for the first time. We stepped outside in the evening, after a day of setting up the house, in time to see a sky full of candlelit lanterns lifting over the beach. The next morning, as we awoke to the sunlight on the pinewood and brightly painted walls, it was more than I'd ever dreamed. The ocean breeze and soft light moved through the rooms. Inspired, I picked up a pad to write. Later, walking barefoot with my youngest son through the grassy dunes above the ocean, I let myself enjoy the *celebration* of a creative dream come true. My son said, "This is the best day ever." "Yes, it is," I whispered into the air.

Making a beach cottage retreat was a dream come true, but it was an understanding of creative rhythms and a routine practice of being creative that brought it into form. Now the form of the dream itself would be a place for *restoration* and further inspiration. As a natural force, creativity replenishes its reservoir.

This Is Your Creative Life

The phrases "Follow your dreams" and "This life is not a dress rehearsal" have been repeated so often they have become clichés, yet there are tools that can enable you to reach for your dreams and make the most of your life. There is the realm of dreams, spirit, and pure potential, and then there is the realm of body, daily life, and the physical reality you live in. Bringing energy from the dream realm to the physical one requires building a bridge between these realms; creativity is the bridge to help anchor the potential of dreams in the body and to embody what we are capable of. We can go into the energy field, where what is not yet formed resides, and shift it or align with it to assist our dream making.

Why are some dreams elusive? This is the mystery that is also part of the creative process. Perhaps the time is not right or the bridge is not strong enough yet. Even the busyness of life can distract from the making of dreams. Having a daily creative practice to engage your resonance and taking time to routinely ponder and focus on your dreams are the essential ingredients. A daily practice brings creative energy to the physical realm of your day-to-day life, and knowing your dreams keeps them alive in your energy field. In order to realize your dreams, you must have a connection with both their spirit and their body.

Bronnie Ware is an Australian nurse who worked with the dying in hospice for many years. In providing care for patients in the last three to twelve weeks of their lives, she found a common theme of regret among them. She wrote about these regrets in a blog that received so much attention that she compiled them into a book: *The Top Five Regrets of the Dying*. The most common were

1. I wish I'd had the courage to live a life true to myself, not the life others expected of me.
2. I wish I hadn't worked so hard. (She heard this from every male patient that she nursed, and especially that they missed their children's youth and their partner's companionship).
3. I wish I'd had the courage to express my feelings.
4. I wish I'd stayed in touch with my friends.
5. I wish I'd let myself be happier.[29]

At the end of life, no one thinks about how much money or professional success they have made. Rather, they examine whether they lived their dreams or not, whether the life they lived gave expression to the desires of the spirit, and whether they were able to share this true aspect of themselves with those they loved. Not one person will regret having spent time on living out their creative dreams because those dreams give voice to the soul.

Exercise: Committing to Your Creative Dreams

Too often, we keep our dreams to ourselves and give them less energy by doing so. Practice this next exercise for ritualizing and sharing your dreams. (You'll need a pen and paper.)

1. Write down your current creative dreams on a piece of paper. Let yourself truly dream, writing even the most expansive notions that come to mind.

2. Review your list and circle your top three dreams.

3. Reflect on how much of your present life is spent on any or all of these dreams. Are the top three visible in your daily life currently? If yes, could they be even more so? If no, how could you redirect your focus toward them?

4. Invite a trusted person to do the above steps of this exercise, then share your dreams with one another by reading them aloud. Reflect on what you have expressed together.

5. Exchange your list of top-three dreams. Then take the dream seeds of the other and plant this paper somewhere in the earth—a symbol honoring the seeds' potential. When we plant and nurture each other's seeds, we tend to our own as well. By working together, our individual dreams are held by the greater energies and resources of the community.

Connecting to the Divine

If we consider creativity a process of bringing spirit into form, then by its nature, it can be considered a divine process—though a uniquely personal one. I was struck by the exploration of creative success and the divine in a *Wall Street Journal* article by Neil Strauss titled "God at the Grammys: The Chosen Ones." He examined the connection between fame, success, and a belief in a higher power. In the article, Lady Gaga says of her success, "It's hard to chalk it all up to myself . . . [There's] a higher power that's been watching out for me." Strauss shares similar responses from Christina Aguilera and then her mom, who says, "Early on I realized . . . God has plans for her." And another one from Snoop Dogg, who says "God makes everything happen."[30]

Strauss initially thought that perhaps attributing success to God was a sign of humility or gratitude, but then he found a common thread among many famous pop stars he researched: they routinely believed God wanted them to be famous. Conversely, Strauss interviewed equally talented but less famous musicians and found a common thread in them: a feeling that their success was accidental or undeserved. They tended to fall out of the limelight. In his mind, it was not necessarily the hand of God but the belief that God wanted them to succeed that was a predictor of real success. Strauss found a similar theme of attributing athletic outcomes to God among successful athletes, such as Green Bay Packers quarterback Aaron Rodgers, who was MVP of the Super Bowl and said, "God always has a plan for us."[31]

Not only was this belief in divine intention a predictor of success, but a connection to the divine also provided refuge from the intensity of fame. As Strauss wrote, "It helps . . . to have a sense of divine mission and to feel that, when everyone else seems to be against you, God is walking on your side. Most stars who feel even a sliver of doubt about being in the spotlight will tend to buckle under the constant pressure. Fearing criticism or failure, they become risk-averse and pass up opportunities." He relayed the difficulties of hip-hop star Sean "P. Diddy" Combs, who had been in and out of jail. When Strauss asked him if he ever felt fear, Diddy replied, "My faith is in God. Like, look who I'm rolling with. Look who my gang really is. My gang is God. Come on, now, I don't have fear." Strauss concludes, "Talent counts for a lot, but so, too, does the motivating power of divine connection."[32]

From an energy perspective, a connection to the divine accesses a far broader energy field. Perhaps in allowing the divine to direct their careers, these celebrities are receiving guidance and inspiration made possible by its pure potential. I see this when working with the energy of my clients: when they focus on their stress and worries (as if they are theirs alone to deal with), the energy around them takes on a contracted pattern. When they settle on their dreams and hopes, the energy has more of an aligned and peaceful quality. And when they place stress, worry, or difficulties into the expanded capacity of the divine—like giving their problems to God—the energy constriction of their burdens dissipates.

When comparing the effects of focused worry and focused intentions during a session, clients notice the difference in their energy fields. And when they call upon spirit to hold either stress or intentions in whatever way spirit is defined for them—a divine presence, inner blessings, the spaciousness associated with a place in nature, a feeling of love—the whole energy in the room is noticeably altered and amplified to a harmonic state. Observing this simple transformation while working with clients' creative energy inspired the diagram for this potential between the interface of body and spirit in our creative fields (see the diagram of the creative-energy field on page 37).

When we align our energy with the greater realm of spirit, we step into the potential of magic, dreams, ancestors, synchronicity, unseen assistance, and the expanded creative capacity of the divine; we take our individual resonance and join with the vast resonance of the whole creative-energy field. To me, this is the power of prayer—not to achieve a particular goal or outcome, but rather to draw from the greater capacity of the divine field. My middle son, Gabe, said to me, "Prayers don't work," because he had prayed for his younger brother not to have a ruptured appendix, and it was ruptured anyway. I explained to him my understanding of prayer: it's not a linear process but a type of energy resonance. Though his prayer might not have prevented the health crisis itself, it certainly brought divine energy to hold his brother and our family through the long journey of healing. When we understand how to work with the divine field, we align our personal energy resonance with the greater field. Then we become one with a potential beyond ours alone.

Energy Session: Soulful Working of the Heart

Mark came for an energy session during a time of transition in his life. He had been divorced for two years after finally leaving his wife, who had been angry and critical throughout their relationship. He had been unhappy during the entire marriage, and once he left the relationship, he had more clarity. His wife had embodied similar patterns to those of his parents, and he recognized in himself the tendency to feel like he somehow deserved a continuous barrage of criticism.

After leaving his marriage, Mark had joined a men's group, where he realized how many unmet needs for validation and recognition he had in himself. He began to learn about his role in identifying and meeting these needs, both for himself and in a relationship. And he came to me for an energy session to support this process—to assist him in developing his capacity for a new intimate relationship.

Mark had found a kind and receptive partner. His challenge was that he found himself sabotaging his ability to receive this offering because he was unused to having it. Unless core patterns that limit flow of energy are changed, a person will find it difficult to embody new potential. For example, Mark likely cocreated a toxic marriage where criticism was the primary exchange of energy because that felt normal to him from his childhood imprints. It's typically not enough to change partners. Unless he changed the core pattern so that he could receive loving exchanges, these interactions would feel uncomfortable and have the potential to sabotage a valued relationship. Criticism and anger contract the energy field, in both the giver and the receiver; they contract the energy around the heart and cut off the flow of love. If Mark frequently witnessed this in his parents, directed toward him or others in the family field, it likely began to feel normal, even if unhealthy. This is how we often pick partners who reflect the limitations of our family fields: unless we are conscious about changing or healing, we tend to choose what we know.

As Mark was talking about his previous marriage, I invited him to notice the tension in his body and the contracted state of his energy field. When he thought about his parents' critical way of communicating, his energy field contracted again. Then I had him do the "Creating a Resonant Energy Field" exercise (page 198). After establishing resonance in his field, Mark realized that for much of his marriage (and much of his childhood), he had lived in a contracted state, cut off from the divine flow of love. I invited him to call to mind his new partner. Initially his energy field contracted again, but this time it was because he did not feel worthy of the positive attention from her; it seemed foreign to his being. I relayed the story from Elizabeth Gilbert's *Eat, Pray, Love* in which she meets the love of her life and initially shuts down in his presence, because the fullness of love he offers is too much for her system. Her inner circuitry was wired for less love, so she had to do the work of expanding her capacity to receive more. When we remember ourselves as sacred—a part of the divine—giving and receiving love are natural expressions of that divinity.

Mark thought about what he wanted for himself and reaffirmed the resonance in his center. He recognized the resistance in his own field to receiving what he wanted, but with this clear awareness, he knew that it would no longer limit him. Mark laughed, "I guess I'll just have to practice receiving her love until I've got it down. Life is pretty good when that's my assignment." Armed with resonance in his center, Mark set off to receive the blessings that come with such soulful working of the heart.

Exercise: Energizing a Dream

Ponder the creative dreams of your heart and choose one for the following exercise. (You will need a pen and paper.)

1. Write an intention for this dream, being as specific as possible. Prepare to read it each morning or night for the next thirty days.
2. Each time you read your intention, notice the patterns of creative flow that arise or help this intention along in some way. Look for patterns of synchronicity to guide your creative process during this month, such as invitations, conversations, things that offer you direction.
3. Also notice any places of resistance—reactions in your body or unexpected challenges to realizing your dream. See these resistance

patterns as potential areas for growth, and bring in resources to help you move from resistance to potential, such as healers, prayers, rituals, books, friends, your own intuition, and so on.

4. Draw upon the masculine or the feminine to further energize this intention. The masculine aspect works directly on creating your dream and takes action in the creation of the dream. The feminine aspect receives guidance and inspiration or calls in dream assistance. See how you might draw upon both fields to energize your dream.

5. Each day, when you read your intention, surround it with love, hope, and blessings. You contain the power, spirit, and joy of a wild creative to manifest your dreams.

Key aspects to remember:

• Dream manifestation begins with setting an intention.
• After setting an intention, watch for signs.
• Prepare for resistance. Resistance can be a natural part of creative expansion.
• Rather than engage resistance, sense the direction of flow.
• Cultivate resonance in your whole creative field (to move through resistance, read the signs, and give form to your dreams).

Your Spirit-Body Interface: Setting the Stage for Miracles

Marianne Williamson, mind-body-spirit teacher and author, defines a miracle as a shift in perception from fear to love. We can also think of this as a shift from a contracted energy field (fear contracts energy) to a resonant energy field (love expands and aligns energy). Ponder the meaning of a miracle and the miracles you have witnessed.

What you are making in your life reveals the state of your relationship between spirit and body. Whatever is in your energy field will be reflected in your life and the creations you are making. Life is the flow; you are the form. Working with your inner creative map as an interface between spirit and body, you can refine these spirit–body forms and set the stage for miracles:

What is sacred?
Where do your dreams reside?
What lies at the heart of your life?
What will you make?
How will you share it?

Life is like this: we accept an invitation, we celebrate with spirit, and we encounter the truth that reveals its meaning to us over time. We may return again and again to comprehend all that we have been given. Embracing the wild creative allows us to move consciously through each cycle and receive the blessings in doing so.

Spirit is the alchemist. In its presence, the mundane becomes magical. What we typically call a miracle is a momentary glimpse of this way of being in life; and the truth is that we ourselves are a miracle of expression.

In the words of poet Mary Oliver, "Tell me, what is it you plan to do with your one wild and precious life?"[33] Let your wild creative give the answer.

CLOSING

Freeing the Wild Within

The language of spirit is not easily understood by the mind. After that first visit from the eagle along the place where the river meets the sea, I purchased an elkskin hand drum and began to make regular pilgrimages to the water to drum with my children. In the drumming and the wild, I found an expanded field of energy that revived my creative current and enabled me to write freely. Yet, as I wrote and came closer to finishing my book, I still had no idea how to publish it.

Finally, with a complete manuscript in hand, I took the heavy sheaf of paper along with my boys and my drum to the ocean. After making a small fire, I set the full manuscript on the sand. I had a manuscript, but nowhere to bring it into book form. I began to drum with a bit of attitude: *Okay, spirit, here's my finished writing. I followed your guidance to "just write" this book. I wrote. I'm done. Here's the manuscript. So now what?* After I spoke these words, a flock of seagulls streamed past. Behind them came several larger birds. I looked up to see three eagles flying over my head—a mother and her two young offspring. I was there with my two boys, and spirit came in the form of a mother

eagle and two young. I was also pregnant with my third son. I dropped
to my knees; this was my answer. I watched them circle overhead.

My oldest son pointed to the sky: "Mama, more eagles."

"I see, honey," I said, my voice a whisper.

The boys played together, running down the soft hillside. The eagles
circled overhead and then alighted on a tall cedar at the edge of the cove.

I lifted my head to the three eagles sitting in the tree and then
turned back to my boys. I felt energy moving through my center, from
spirit to body—from the realm of spirit to the earthen plane where we
sat. A mother eagle, a human mother. From spirit to body we come,
and from body to spirit we will return. I sat in the peace and contentment of my spirit, at ease in the place of all things. Tears spilled down
both sides of my face, making tiny wet drops on the sand. My sense
of being bound by time and the confines of my body fell away, and I
entered a spaciousness of sound and light.

Then, just as they had come, the eagles took flight again, circling
overhead once more before turning out across the rocks and rolling
waves to a place beyond our sight. I pounded my message of *thank you*
on the drum, the sound echoing after them on the sea. Eventually, I
packed my drum, the manuscript, my children, and my own self back
into the car and turned us toward home. I still had no idea how to proceed, but once again, I had received an energy that bolstered my faith
and my trust in the workings of spirit.

Though I had received a message—one that registered in the core
of my body—my logical mind wanted more. I thought of Russell, a
man who travels through our neighborhood and rests under the shade
of a giant walnut tree near our house. He is a gentle soul who intentionally lives on the street. When the sorrowful sounds of a harmonica
float to our door, we know that Russell is nearby. A native Tlingit,
Russell was raised by his grandmother, a respected medicine woman,
in rural Alaska. He and I had talked several times about his experience
with the wild as a boy, and he told me of his lineage from the eagle clan.

After these encounters with eagles in the wild, I longed to speak with someone who had a personal connection to the eagle spirit. Russell walked by one evening while I was playing with my sons on the front lawn. There was an eagle imprinted on his shirt, and I pointed to it. Russell answered by saying, "My Tlingit name means 'eagle looking into a body of water.'" I told him about our first encounter with the eagle at the river's edge and the second one, with the mother and two young eagles. Russell surprised me by saying we were blessed. He asked if he could touch me.

I started to ask more questions, wondering if there was more that I should know, but Russell reached his hand toward mine. I remembered my breath. He was telling me not to go looking for something that I already had. Through the presence of another, spirit was again answering my prayer. Perhaps this is how it is: we search for something, we ask for a blessing, and we find it has already been received if we are able to see what has been given. The opening passed as quickly as it had come. I nodded my head to Russell, then turned to gather my children toward sleep. That night, I dreamt of birds and flight.

The last eagle encounter came on a wet winter day. I had taken the medicine from the wild and continued to weave its energy into a self-published book. I mothered my sons and gave birth to my third son. I followed the directions from spirit that led to each milestone while also integrating our newest family member. A year and a half later, in early November, a single copy of the finished book arrived at my door. A few days after the book's arrival, I awoke with the impulse to give thanks at the ocean. I gathered the book, my three sons, and my drum into the car, and we drove through thickets of rain to the ocean. I almost turned home, realizing that the winter weather would cut short our time there, but instead followed the stronger inner current.

Arriving at the ocean's edge, my boys and I leaned into the wind. I held my youngest son, wrapped in a wool shawl. The rain dispersed, but the cold fog blew around our feet. We walked quickly through the dunes and the chilled brush of ocean air to the opening above the sea. Together, we looked down to see an eagle feasting on a brown pelican at the water's edge. Words came to me: *Your offering has been received; spirit is fed.*

We stood just briefly. Before fleeing the cold, my oldest son said, "Mom, another eagle."

"Yes," I replied, as if eagles were an everyday occurrence in our lives, and a shiver of gratitude moved through my body. I sensed that one of my life tasks had been completed; I had the impression we were saying good-bye. Indeed, I have never seen another eagle in this way, though I have been to these same beaches many times since. Once, when I asked about this, I heard, *You carry this energy within you now. Perhaps eagle is visiting another wild creative, like you, in another wild place, in response to a call for spirit.*

Place your creative dreams in the deeper currents,
where spirit meets body,
and they will become real.
See that the beauty in these dreams
is you.

Acknowledgments

Dreams really can come true, but not without the assistance of a good team and gifts of spirit. The beauty of making your dreams real is that it's an opportunity to engage the creative field with others.

One of the essential dream weavers for this book has been Cynthia Black. Thank you, Cynthia, for being one of the original wild creatives, a great mother to so many, and for dreaming so well—*aloha* always.

Thank you to Beyond Words publisher, Richard Cohn, and Atria Books publisher, Judith Curr, for visionary publishing and cocreating these books. To the exceptional team of cocreators for weaving words into book form: Jenefer Angell, Emily Han, Lindsay S. Brown, Devon Smith, Emmalisa Sparrow, Bill Brunson, Whitney Quon, Leah Brown, and Jackie Hooper.

Thank you to the women (and men) in my practice for sharing, exploring, and stepping into your dreams as we discover the power of the body's creative energy. To all the wild creatives, I celebrate your beauty. May you shine the light so others can follow.

Blessings to the healers who have restored the vibrant flow of energy in my own creative field.

To my family and parents, I am thankful for the powerful creative current that runs through our line. Thank you for using it to transform what you were given.

Thank you to my early friends, teachers, and other influences who encouraged me to dream and create—especially to those who teach the arts and value creativity in all its forms. Gratitude for one of my favorite dream creators, Nancy Cook, and her dream child, Izi.

To my book club and tribe—Jen, Michelle, Mary, Neha, Holly, Brooke, Tali, and Sara—I am thankful for our practice over the years of gathering to nourish and encourage one another, and for celebrating dreams that come true. Dreams are best when shared.

For Sara DeLuca and Jan Kent, you are part of my most cherished dreams. May we continue to dream and savor these dreams together.

To my chief dream maker and cocreator, Dan Kent: "No matter how many times we meet, it's not enough." You are the dream of my heart. Thank you for inspiring and collaborating on this dream life we are making.

To my beautiful sons, Nick, Gabe, and Japhy: you are dreams come true, each one of you. Always remember the beauty in your center. Stay near the creative channel that is your birthright. And if you forget, your daddy and I will remind you, because we witnessed the power, spirit, and joy of your entry. We see you. We're so very glad that you came.

To Kiva, Moka, Kona, Ollie, and Magoo—animal friends: thank you for tending the earth and the spirit creative field of our family.

And to the spirits of the land—my spirit daughter, the ancestors, and eagle—I give thanks. Always, deep gratitude to the wild feminine for keeping me company through the dark nights and inspired days, winter and summer, nursing babies and tending children, writing and going to the wild, and whispering words by the fire. You are loved. I'll meet you at the ocean.

Appendix

List of Exercises

Notes

1. David Whyte, "Sweet Darkness," *The House of Belonging* (Langley, WA: Many Rivers Press, 1997), 23.

2. David Whyte, *The Three Marriages: Reimagining Work, Self, and Relationship* (New York: Riverhead Books, 2009), 150.

3. Amnon Buchbinder, "Out of Our Heads: Philip Shepherd On the Brain in Our Belly," *The Sun*, no. 448 (April 2013), http://thesunmagazine.org/issues/448/out_of_our_heads.

4. The Centre for Bhutan Studies & GNH Research website, "GNH: Concept," accessed July 2012, http://www.grossnationalhappiness.com/articles/.

5. Marion Woodman, *Bone: Dying into Life* (New York: Viking Penguin, 2000), 61.

6. Danielle LaPorte, *The Desire Map: A Guide to Creating Goals with Soul* (Boulder, CO: Sounds True, 2014), 7.

7. Marie Forleo, "Live Your Purpose with Marie Forleo and Mastin Kipp," MarieTV, MarieForleo.com, June 4, 2012, http://www.marieforleo.com/2012/06/live-your-purpose/.

8. "Brené Brown: The Power of Vulnerability," TED talks, December 23, 2010, http://www.ted.com/talks/brene_brown_on_vulnerability.html.

9. "Brené Brown: Listening to Shame," TED talks, March 16, 2012, http://www
   .ted.com/talks/brene_brown_listening_to_shame.html.

10. Brené Brown, *Daring Greatly: How the Courage to Be Vulnerable Transforms the
    Way We Live, Love, Parent, and Lead* (New York: Gotham Books, 2012), 1.

11. "Brené Brown: Listening to Shame."

12. Nathan Tucker, "Schoolhouse Electric's Founder Escapes from the Digital World,"
    Portland Monthly, January 21, 2014, http://www.portlandmonthlymag.com/style
    -and-shopping/lookbook/articles/brian-fahertys-analog-refuge-january-2014.

13. Deepak Chopra, *The Seven Spiritual Laws of Success: A Practical Guide to the Ful-
    fillment of Your Dreams* (Novato, CA: New World Library, 1994), 22.

14. Mary Mazzio, "What Richard Branson's Mother Taught Me About Raising
    Entrepreneurial Kids," *Huffington Post*, July 24, 2012, http://www.huffington
    post.com/young-entrepreneur-council/what-i-learned-from-richa_b_1696734
    .html?utm_hp_ref=tw.

15. David Wagoner, "Lost," *Traveling Light: Collected and New Poems* (Champaign,
    IL: University of Illinois Press, 1999), 10.

16. William Stafford, "You Reading This, Be Ready," *The Way It Is: New and Selected
    Poems* (Minneapolis: Graywolf Press, 1998), 45.

17. Robert Cole and Paul Williams, *The Book of Houses* (Kingsport, Tennessee: Ent-
    whistle Books, 1980).

18. Nassim Nicholas Taleb, "Learning to Love Volatility," *The Wall Street Journal*,
    November 16, 2012, http://online.wsj.com/news/articles/SB100014241278873
    24735104578120953311383448.

19. Ibid.

20. Seth Godin, *The Icarus Deception: How High Will You Fly?* (New York: Portfolio
    Penguin, 2012), 1.

21. Deva Daricha, "The Making of a Shaman," accessed July 2012, http://human
    transformation.com.au/store/books/product/show/1-the-making-of-a-shaman
    /category_pathway-12.

22. Tilth Producers of Washington website, "Jello Mold Farm: Diane Szukovathy & Dennis Westphall Member Spotlight," April 2011, http://tilthproducers.org /mom/april-2011/.

23. Diane Szukovathy, personal communication with the author, November 1, 2013.

24. Angus Loten, "Search for Doctor Leads to Yelp," *The Wall Street Journal*, November 14, 2012, http://online.wsj.com/news/articles/SB100014241278873245959 04578117512589717352.

25. Betsy Hammond, "Earthquakes and Portland-Area Schools: New Safety Approach Draws Attention," *The Oregonian*, November 1, 2012, http://www.oregonlive .com/education/index.ssf/2012/11/earthquakes_and_portland-area.html.

26. D. K. Row, "Brad Swift Does It All to Make His Portland Bee Balm," *The Oregonian*, October 22, 2012, http://www.oregonlive.com/small-business/index.ssf /2012/10/brad_swift_does_it_all_to_make.html.

27. Jake Coyle, "As a Bond Villain, Bardem Gives 'Skyfall' a Jolt," Associated Press, October 23, 2012, http://bigstory.ap.org/article/bond-villain-bardem-gives-sky fall-jolt.

28. Louise Hay, "Your Thoughts Create Your Tomorrows," March 4, 2013, http:// www.healyourlife.com/author-louise-l-hay/2013/03/lifehelp/success-and -abundance/your-thoughts-create-your-tomorrows.

29. Bronnie Ware, "Top 5 Regrets of the Dying," *Huffington Post*, January 21, 2012, http://www.huffingtonpost.com/bronnie-ware/top-5-regrets-of-the-dyin_b _1220965.html.

30. Neil Strauss, "God at the Grammys: The Chosen Ones," *The Wall Street Journal*, February 12, 2011, http://online.wsj.com/news/articles/SB1000142405274870 48584045761346011055583860.

31. Ibid.

32. Ibid.

33. Mary Oliver, "The Summer Day," *The Truro Bear and Other Adventures: Poems and Essays* (Boston: Beacon Press, 2008), 94.

Make a nesting now, a place to which
the birds can come, think of Kevin's
prayerful palm holding the blackbird's egg
and be the one, looking out from this place
who warms interior forms into light.
Feel the way the cliff at your back
gives shelter to your outward view
and then bring in from those horizons
all discordant elements that seek a home.

Be taught now, among the trees and rocks,
how the discarded is woven into shelter,
learn the way things hidden and unspoken
slowly proclaim their voice in the world.
Find that far inward symmetry
to all outward appearances, apprentice
yourself to yourself, begin to welcome back
all you sent away, be a new annunciation,
make yourself a door through which
to be hospitable, even to the stranger in you.

See with every turning day,
how each season makes a child
of you again, wants you to become
a seeker after rainfall and birdsong,
watch now, how it weathers you
to a testing in the tried and true,
admonishes you with each falling leaf,
to be courageous, to be something
that has come through, to be the last thing
you want to see before you leave the world.

Above all, be alone with it all,
a hiving off, a corner of silence
amidst the noise, refuse to talk,
even to yourself, and stay in this place
until the current of the story
is strong enough to float you out.

Ghost then, to where others
in this place have come before,
under the hazel, by the ruined chapel,
below the cave where Coleman slept,
become the source that makes
the river flow, and then the sea
beyond. Live in this place
as you were meant to and then,
surprised by your abilities,
become the ancestor of it all,
the quiet, robust and blessed Saint
that your future happiness
will always remember.
—DAVID WHYTE

"Coleman's Bed" from
River Flow: New & Selected Poems, 1984–2007
© 2006 Many Rivers Press